A Handbook
of Behavior
Modification
for the Classroom

Abraham Givner
Paul S. Graubard

Yeshiva University

A Handbook
of Behavior
Modification
for the Classroom

HOLT, RINEHART AND WINSTON, INC.
New York   Chicago   San Francisco   Atlanta
Dallas   Montreal   Toronto   London   Sydney

Cartoons by Isauro de la Rosa

Library of Congress Cataloging in Publication Data

Givner, Abraham.
    A handbook of behavior modification for the classroom.

    1. Teaching. 2. Behaviorism (Psychology)
I. Graubard, Paul S., joint author. II. Title.
LB1025.2.G56   371.1'02   73-22335

ISBN: 0-03-006941-6

To Debbie and Joy

Preface

"Spare the rod, use behavior mod!" is an interesting idea provoked by the continued acceptance and recognition of the value of behavior modification techniques in the classroom by the general public and by teachers, parents, administrators, educators, and students themselves.

Behavior modification has been catapulted into the headlines of newspapers, professional journals, television documentaries, and talk shows across the country because of its success. It has succeeded where other educational methods have failed; it has not only succeeded in helping the student learn but, in many cases, it has helped him reach levels previously considered unattainable. It has succeeded with children who were labeled autistic, schizophrenic, juvenile delinquent, brain damaged, retarded, or disadvantaged; more currently it has been used with exemplary success with "normal" children. Behavior modification has been used by teachers, parents, administrators, researchers, and psychologists to better the environment we live in, and to help the student learn more effectively in that environment.

This book is designed for use by teachers. It is based upon our daily experiences with teaching and with teachers who have used behavior modification methods. It is dedicated to the philosophy that "left to himself in a given environment a student will learn, but he will not necessarily have been taught. The school of experience is no school at all, not because no one learns in it but because no one teaches. Teaching is the expediting of learning; a person who is taught learns more quickly than one who is not" (Skinner, p. 5). In other words, let us not leave to accidental occurrences what a child learns; let us make use of the most effective methods available for teaching. This manual describes those methods; the authors believe that behavior modification or behavior analysis techniques provide an effective way of teaching.

In two recent reviews of the literature concerning behavior modification in schools (O'Leary & Drabman, 1971; Bushell & Brigham, 1971), the authors *failed to find a single case where token systems*, one form of behavior modification, *were ineffective*. These systems have become so effective that they have been attacked—attacked as being too effective! The cry goes up that the children are not treated as children but as nonthinking robots, and the teacher is made into an M&M dispenser.

It is sad that this has occurred because it is truly a distortion of the facts.* We are now in an age of technological advancement and excitement in education. It is not only the educators who are excited, it is the students who are no longer bored with school, who see some tangible results from their work, and who sense they are on the threshold of new discoveries. It is the student who doesn't close his books the moment the bell rings, but who stays after class, not as a punishment, but because he enjoys what is happening in class. It is the student who learns that cooperation with peers is an

---

* These facts are examined in great detail in an exciting new book entitled *Cooperative Classroom Management* by Robert Williams and Kamala Anandam (Columbus, Ohio: Charles E. Merrill Publishing Co., 1973).

easier way of getting ahead than fighting. It is the student who has learned that the rod is no longer hanging over his head. Learning can become exciting and functional, and behavior modification techniques can aid in this quest.

Reports describing reinforcement programs in the professional literature are usually accompanied by tables, graphs, statistical analyses, results, and discussions. Most of these reports, however, do not tell you how to do it. This book is intended to be a handbook with general principles and specific techniques. Its purpose is to enable you to apply, in the classroom, the latest available teaching technology, which has proved effective in changing children's behavior and in promoting learning.

All of the techniques described here were successfully employed in public elementary schools. Most of the examples were also taken from public school cases. Some of them have also been tried out in alternative school settings with equal success. The school setting can vary, but the problems are usually the same: How do you teach academic skills and concepts? How do you teach useful and relevant social skills? How do you teach people to be objective and self-critical and to read their environment accurately? The structure and atmosphere might differ, but free schools and more traditional private schools face the same critical teaching problems that public schools do. The problems raised in teachers' lounges sound quite similar across the country. Teachers are searching for answers because they recognize that their effectiveness needs to be considerably improved. The methods detailed in this book can help you improve your teaching performance, and it is to this end that this book was written.

Many teachers are aware of the powerful effects that reinforcement programs have had on classrooms, or at least they are aware of the literature describing these effects. Nevertheless, they are reluctant to try out aspects of these programs. This reluctance can be traced to two main factors. First, there are serious ethical concerns about instituting such systems: teachers have many unanswered questions concerning the wisdom of using behavior modification techniques. Second, they don't know how to implement these procedures. We believe that the "how to do it" sections give the cogent answers to philosophical misgivings.

It will be found that behavior modification does not reduce children and/or teachers to automatons, nor are these methods by their very nature repressive. Rather, they can be used to reach any goal that teachers and students can agree upon. We have added a chapter discussing the most frequently asked questions about behavior modification, but we feel that learning by example is more effective than learning by discussion, and so we have put that chapter last.

This book could never have been completed without the able assistance of Edith Friedman. We owe her our heartfelt thanks. Debbie Givner tried out the procedures described in this book and helped us immensely, as did Selma Katz of P.S. 145M in New York City, who gave us the administrative cooperation necessary to try out the methodology. Katy Le-Laurin, Gila Stamler, Fran Alter, and Linda Forman of Yeshiva University were especially helpful with their criticism, as were Tom and Joan Brigham of Western Washington University. Don Bushell, Jr., was also most helpful with his suggestions.

November 1973

Abraham Givner
Paul S. Graubard

Contents

A Handbook
of Behavior
Modification
for the Classroom

Chapter I

Eight Guidelines of Reinforcement Systems for Developing Effective Instruction

Behavior modification is not a magical technique.
It is a system that gives you some of the best tools now available with which to teach.

> "Mrs. G., can we come to your house on Friday? Can we play with Caleb the cat and go to the park?
>
> These two girls were in a third-grade class that made use of behavior modification techniques. The girls had been described as being undependable, irresponsible, disruptive, and truant, with a dislike for school and teachers when this program began. Perhaps their reaction to their school situation was valid, but it was not productive for themselves, their peers, or their teachers.
>
> Now, three months later, you can picture the change for yourself. Where is that "overly aggressive, tough, school-hating, predelinquent nine-year-old terror"? Where is that child who was expelled three times last year? Where is that child who had been promoted only because she couldn't be held over again? The two girls know that on Friday Mrs. G. takes children to her home as a "reward" for schoolwork and appropriate behavior. They know how to get the credits to go to Mrs. G.'s house. What did they have to do to get the reward? They had to act in an almost totally opposite manner than they did prior to the onset of the program.

Modifying behavior is not easy, but it can be done. You can't expect a disruptive child to be quiet by waving a lollipop in front of him—though some teachers try it. What is needed is an understanding of a few principles of behavior and reinforcement and many specific techniques.

Once you are familiar with these principles and have followed the instructions for setting up your own programs, you will find that you have greater flexibility and skill in handling specific problems that may arise in your classrooms. Such ability is necessary, for the systems presented here will not be the answer to all your classroom problems. It will be necessary for you to modify them and tailor them to your own classroom needs.

"Reinforcement" has been a frequently used term in discussions on current trends in education. These discussions take place in teachers' lounges as well as in college classrooms. But just as frequently, reinforcement has been misinterpreted and misused. What are reinforcers? What do they look like? Where do you find them? How do you use them once they are found?

This first chapter will define terms, discuss certain key principles of reinforcement, describe procedures for implementing reinforcement systems, and illustrate several cases in which they have been applied. This format is used so that the principles of reinforcement theory will be understood, and systems will not be applied mechanically and/or incorrectly.

In reality, what a teacher does is more important than what a teacher wants to do. A teacher might want to set up a reinforcement system, but if the timing of delivering a reinforcement is off, or if a teacher sets his goals too high, instead of reinforcing approximations of behavior, the reinforcement system may not be effective or, worse, will help to shape behaviors that will be deleterious for both the child and the teacher. Therefore, understanding of the principles involved in behavior modification can be quite helpful to both teacher and student. These principles will be explained in the discussion of the eight guidelines of reinforcement systems for managing classroom behavior that follows.

GUIDELINE 1

A reinforcer is defined by its ability to accelerate, or increase, the rate at which a behavior will occur. Do not think that simply giving a child a reward will increase or strengthen any particular behavior. It is more complex than that. What behavior is to be reinforced and when it is to be reinforced will be major determinants of any reinforcement program. The reinforcer must be made contingent on the behavior to be reinforced (that is, there must be a *relationship* between the specific response and the consequences that response evokes from the environment), and the reinforcer should not be delivered *until* the specific behavior is made overt. Contingencies are the key to reinforcement systems. A contingency is an if–then proposition. If the behavior is emitted or made overt, then it is reinforced, and the more it is reinforced the more it will recur.

A typical classroom example can serve as a departure point for discussing the principles of behavior modification:

> "Billy, sit down. You're not supposed to be out of your seat! Now sit down and open your book. We're waiting for you."
>
> Billy idles back to his seat while the teacher watches, and he begins to open his book. The class returns to its lesson. Two minutes pass. Billy goes over to Eddie and they begin talking to each other, disturbing those children who are trying to read.
>
> "Billy and Eddie, stop talking. You're disturbing everyone."
>
> Taking their cue from the teacher, everyone turns to see what Billy and Eddie are doing. Twenty-five curious faces are now attending to Billy and Eddie. (Without a doubt, instances such as these occur in every teacher's classroom at least once a day.)

Could the teacher and peer attention have served as a *reinforcer* in both of these examples? From these two interactions it would be impossible to state a definitive answer, but it is highly probable that the teacher's attention and perhaps peer attention were reinforcers in these cases. Remember

Guideline 1: a reinforcer increases, or accelerates, the rates at which behaviors will occur again in the future. Billy was out of the seat and was able to get the teacher's attention by an inappropriate behavior. Billy then sat down, received no attention from the teacher, and began talking to his friend—receiving peer attention. This interaction was *immediately* followed by the teacher's attention once again. In both instances *teacher attention* followed inappropriate behavior. It is highly probable that Billy will again display this same kind of behavior (this in fact did happen in this particular classroom) because his teacher responds and attends to these behaviors, and did not give him work which he found more reinforcing than interrupting lessons.

Why does Billy want the teacher's attention? Why does teacher attention act as a reinforcer? Such questions can only be answered in a hypothetical manner, since we cannot be certain of the answer. Perhaps Billy is "starved" for adult attention, either positive or negative. Perhaps he "loves" the teacher and does not want her attending to other students. Perhaps being able to get the teacher's attention demonstrates Billy's power in the class. Although Billy's motive can only be guessed at, we can find out the effect such an event as attention has on behavior.

Teacher attention is a broad term that denotes many kinds of teacher behaviors. Hugging, patting, talking, yelling, pushing, and hitting are all examples of teacher attention. They can all be positive reinforcers, as they can all increase the frequency of a child's behavior. If, over a period of time, a child cannot elicit a teacher's attention (being called on) by appropriate behavior, he will probably display an inappropriate behavior, such as cursing, which may get a rise out of the teacher. Even if the teacher yells at him for this and he stops cursing for a while, he has succeeded in getting the teacher's attention. Again, we don't know why it is reinforcing (we are on much safer ground scientifically in discussing relationships rather than causes), nor will the cause affect our system. Yelling is often reinforcing, and students will produce a diversity of behaviors to get this type of attention from the teacher.

Hiding in the closet, running out of the room, fighting, throwing chairs across the room, yelling, cursing, and making noise can all be inappropriate attention-seeking events. Raising a hand, completing an arithmetic assignment, and cooperating are also attention-seeking behaviors that can be appropriate, and if they are they should be reinforced. As a teacher it is your responsibility to work with the child and decide which behaviors you want to increase and which you want to decrease. Only the overt behaviors can be worked with, with any degree of precision.

The fact that the teacher's attention is forthcoming after each inappropriate behavior can increase the probability that Billy will again emit a similar behavior. Similarly, the absence of attention while Billy is sitting quietly can decrease the probability of that behavior being emitted. In this case it can be surmised that teacher attention increased the rate of emitting the inappropriate behavior. (For Billy, teacher attention is probably a reinforcer.) But the only way to be sure of this conclusion is to continue observing the teacher and the pupil in the classroom. (Methods of observation are discussed in detail in Chapter 4.) Of course, incidents in the classroom are not always so clear-cut. They often involve several factors. Nevertheless, the ability of teacher actions to accelerate the rate of pupil behavior, as shown in our example, can be observed in most classroom situations.

To this point we have discussed one potential reinforcer—teacher attention—and the possible consequences of its use. There are other potential reinforcers that you can locate within your educational environment, if you are astute in observing your students. *Reinforcers are idiosyncratic to each individual, and the child is in the best position to know what he likes. Let him decide that.* The most common mistake that teachers make in setting up reinforcement systems is to choose reinforcers that are pleasing to the teacher but not to the child. For a reinforcement system to be effective, the child should be able to choose his own reinforcer! Three fairly simple methods by which to pinpoint such individually oriented reinforcers are presented below.

Methods of Selecting
Reinforcements

1. Observe what the child likes to do, what he does frequently. Interestingly enough, much of what children like to do would be considered inappropriate in many classrooms. Does he read comics during class? Does he express a desire for a particular academic or vocational subject? Does he frequently talk with the same friends during class? Does he eat food during class? Does he seek the attention of a particular teacher or adult in your environment? Does he leave the classroom without permission consistently? The question of what each child likes will be answered when you observe his behavior. Each answer will give you a clue to a potential reinforcer for that student.
2. Observe what follows specific behaviors. Is a child's leaving the room followed by the teacher's running after him? Are clownish outbursts followed by attention from peers or the teacher? The events that follow behaviors may be reinforcing them, and you can possibly employ them as reinforcers. Recall Guideline 1, that a reinforcer will increase the probability of a behavior occurring again. By observing your responses and peer responses to specific behaviors, you will be able to get additional clues for potential reinforcers.
3. Ask your students what they would like to do with free time, what they would like to have, and what they would like to work for. When you use this method to locate reinforcers, it is advisable to place certain limits on the choices available. The restrictions must be reasonable and should be explained to your students carefully. What are the restrictions? The price of the reinforcer, its legality, its accessibility during the day, and interference with routine daily activities should be considered. Making loud noises during a work period, for example, is probably not acceptable and therefore that should not be an option for your students.

Reinforcing Activities and Equipment   The following is a partial list of reinforcers that you have or can make available in your educational environment.

> Serving as monitor
> Going to the library
> Using a bat and/or ball

Leading a group game
Watering plants
Feeding fish
Going to the park
Learning how to write script
Game time
Talk time
Teacher attention
Ticket to ball game
Comic books
A pair of gloves*
A basketball
Magic Marker
Scout equipment

Children will work to earn pleasurable activities that can be academic or nonacademic, just as adults work for different things at different times.

Consumable Reinforcers Edibles will almost always be reinforcing, except when your students have had abundant food and drink during the school day and are not thirsty or hungry. Since this is a rare occurrence for children or adolescents who are in school for six hours a day, it is a safe venture to use soda, cookies, candy, and other food and drink as reinforcers.

These are just some of the reinforcers available to you for your behavior modification program. As you will note, most of the reinforcers listed here and in Appendix A are usually available in most schools and will not require any expenditure. We have stated that these are all *potential* reinforcers because you will not know whether something is a reinforcer until you have tried it. What is reinforcing for one student is not necessarily reinforcing for another. Therefore it will be advisable for you to review and consider the three methods outlined earlier under "Methods of Selecting Reinforcements" for each student. Guideline 2 describes an effective way of using reinforcers.

_____

* This works especially well in the winter for children who do not have gloves.

GUIDELINE 2

The most advantageous time for dispensing reinforcers is immediately after the desired behavior is emitted. It is important that the child understand immediately what he is being reinforced for, and what behaviors are required of him in the future. For example, a teacher with a class of thirty children might want to have the children raise their hand for permission to speak during a discussion as a part of classroom routines. But in a class of thirty children there is a high probability that students who raise their hands to answer or ask questions are not attended to until some time has passed, by which time their hands have been lowered. If there was no immediate reinforcement for having his hand up, the student may have learned the erroneous lesson: "I will be attended to, reinforced, when my hand is down." It is highly improbable that a teacher can call on each student each time his hand is raised. However, once you decide to reinforce hand raising or any other behavior, you must be consistent and systematic in administering it. Call only on children whose hands are raised, or inform students with raised hands that you see them and you will call on them after the first student has responded. In this manner you are immediately reinforcing the specific behavior.

In classrooms it is quite common to hear students say, "Give me back my ball and I'll sit down." The teacher who complies with these directives and allows her own behavior to be shaped without realizing that she is doing so will repeatedly find herself in similar situations.

That particular form of student negotiation should not be encouraged; moreover, the teacher's behaviors are as subject to the same laws of reinforcement as children's (see p. 21). In this example, the child's tendency to play ball in class and get his ball in return for a promise to sit down will probably increase in frequency. *It is not good practice to mollify and assuage the child who is the most frequently disruptive without thinking through exactly what you are doing.* Doing anything just to get him quiet is not helping to solve the problem but, in reality, can be reinforcing. The proper use of contingency statements, such as "If you sit down and do your work for this period, then you can get your ball," are more useful ways of handling these problems. The arrangement of such contingencies for reinforcement is called _contingency management_.

GUIDELINE 3

Extinction: A behavior that is not followed by reinforcement will decrease, or decelerate, in frequency—it will not occur as often. In the example concerning Billy two appropriate behaviors were emitted. He sat down at his desk and opened his book. The consequences of these acts were inattention from the teacher. This was followed by Billy emitting an inappropriate response. Following Guideline 3, since Billy's appropriate behaviors were not reinforced, the frequency of their occurrence will decrease. If a nonreinforcement situation continues, appropriate behaviors may undergo extinction and may not occur again with any frequency. Similarly, if your paychecks were withheld each week, the probability is very high that your coming to school each day to teach would undergo extinction. You would, in fact, stop coming to school. This example highlights the fact that one method for decreasing the frequency of a behavior is to stop reinforcing it. If, in Billy's case, the teacher had ignored rather than reinforced his inappropriate behavior, the probability of its occurrence would in all likelihood have decreased.

Two important qualifications must, however, be added to this statement. Peer attention could act as a reinforcer, and when behavior is ignored or put on an extinction schedule there is often a temporary increase in the behavior. This is analogous to what many people do when the gum machine does not work after they have put in a coin—they shake or bang on the machine for a few minutes. If the machine continues to ignore them and does not give out the gum, the person gets the message and stops shaking or banging the machine. Thus Billy's behavior will probably not disappear immediately. Quite to the contrary, the inappropriate behavior will probably continue. It is only after repeated interactions, in which you continue to ignore the behavior, that it will decrease to an appreciable extent. By repeated interactions we mean days and perhaps even weeks of such consistent teacher reaction. A behavior, such as cursing, which has been reinforced by teachers, parents, and peers for many years, cannot be expected to disappear after only one or two "correct" reactions. Of course you could probably get the student to sit or be quiet in a much shorter period of time if you yell at him, but that may increase the problem because yelling can reinforce the behavior. Remember Guideline 1. The extinction process takes a long time.

At the same time that you decrease the probability of one behavior, it is advisable to increase the strength of a more desirable *incompatible behavior*. While the teacher is ignoring Billy's disruptive behavior, she should reinforce his appropriate classroom behavior that is incompatible with disruption. For example, sitting quietly at his desk, reading, or answering questions are all behaviors that are incompatible with loud and disruptive talking. This useful technique of reinforcing incompatible behavior will be discussed more fully in Chapter 3.

GUIDELINE 4

Be consistent and systematic. This principle applies not only to the administration of reinforcers but to the management of all the behavior modification programs.

Avoid giving students different messages pertaining to the same behavior. If you fluctuate in your behavior, the students will behave erratically. If on Monday you praise reading responses, on Tuesday you ignore this performance, and on Wednesday you again praise it, children will not be able to discriminate the consequences of their own behavior—that is, they will not be able to predict with accuracy your reaction to their behavior. Since your attention to their behavior can be reinforcing, their behavior is being maintained by a random reinforcer and will consequently lead to random and erratic behavior. However, if you consistently ignore or praise the same behaviors, then both your students and you will have clearer expectations of each other's behaviors. You will be able to put consequences on their responses in the light of your own consistent reactions. Once you initiate one reinforcement pattern, do not fluctuate from it unless you have certain indications that it is not successful. With any change *you should make it perfectly clear to your students that there is a new message that will be consistently and systematically adhered to.*

GUIDELINE 5

Be specific in defining the dimensions of each reinforcer for your students.

1. Specify the *time* of delivery of the reinforcement. That is, when will the reinforcer be administered? For example, "Candy is to be given before lunch and at dismissal time." "Students can take a walk at twelve o'clock." The time, however, should not conflict with regular classroom functioning.
2. Specify the *place* for reinforcement. For example: "Games will be distributed at the teacher's desk at 11:00 A.M." or "Basketball playing is in the gym at 11:00."
3. Specify the *duration* of the reinforcement. "Walks are for fifteen minutes, from 11:00 to 11:15." "Games will be distributed from 11 to 11:10 A.M. at the teacher's desk." When the reinforcement period has terminated, it is most advantageous for the student to return to the academic subject as quickly as possible. That is, it is desirable that the student not linger, or extend the reinforcement period beyond its specified limit. One method of accelerating such a behavior is to reinforce the student for returning to his seat and beginning work without delay.
4. Specify the *administrator* of the reinforcer. The student must know who will administer each type of reinforcement. It is not

necessary for the teacher to personally administer all the reinforcers. For example, the gym teacher can supervise gym activities, observing the time, duration, and activity. Your aide, paraprofessional, or monitor can distribute any specific reinforcers that you decide on. A detailed explanation of this aspect of reinforcement can be found in Ayllon and Azrin (1968).

GUIDELINE 6

When a desired terminal behavior or the duration of that desired behavior is not currently attainable, then reinforcing successive approximations to that desired terminal behavior will eventually lead to the same result. A terminal behavior is defined as the behavior the student will be expected to achieve —for example, dividing polysyllabic words correctly—at the end of your instructional program; the terminal behavior is described in terms of explicit criteria by which the performance will be judged. By not requiring more than the student can do, or causing undue frustration or emotional reaction by setting unattainable interim objectives, by reinforcing your students for what they can do, and by systematically applying the reinforcement principles, your students and therefore your program will be successful.

Before instituting a token economy or any other reinforcement system several factors about your students should be considered. All students in your educational setting will be at different academic and behavioral levels of competence. Your first task is to know where your students are in terms of competence. This is accomplished through observational techniques (discussed in Chapter 4) and through curriculum measures (Chapter 5). Such observations will help you know the deficiencies and proficiencies of each student and thus will help you to deduce a plan of action for your students. For example, if a student has a monitor's job and is caught fighting with some other students, he may try to avoid the negative consequences by lying to the teacher and telling her that he did not start the fight. If the teacher believes him, he will have avoided the negative consequences—which in this case was calling in his parents. He has learned that lying is an effective method for avoiding aversive consequences. He has been reinforced for lying and will continue to do so in the future. Similarly *avoiding negative consequences* in the classroom is reinforcing. A student may leave the room without permission during each math period. This may indicate that he is avoiding negative consequences. Being in the class during math is aversive and he tries to avoid it by leaving the class during that period. In planning the program objectives for this student, you should consider his avoidance behavior.

There are *terminal objectives*—those to be achieved by the end of your program—and *interim objectives*—goals that must be achieved on the road to the terminal objective. If a student is out of his seat 95 percent of the time and completes only 5 percent of his work, a terminal goal for him may be to be seated 95 percent of the time and to complete 95 percent of the work correctly. To expect him to show that much appropriate behavior at the outset of your program is inviting failure. Reinforcement of *successive approximations* to the terminal objective will help him to reach the goal. You cannot expect him to be seated for a full hour before you reinforce him; such a long period of proper behavior may never spontaneously occur. Remember that the most advantageous time for reinforcing behavior is immediately after the desired behavior is emitted. If you have observed that he can sit, attend, and work for 5 consecutive minutes, then initially reinforce him after that length of time. When he is able to stay seated and work for a slightly longer period of time, set your criterion for reinforcement at that level. He is now to be reinforced after 10 minutes of appropriate behavior. The student must be informed of this change in criterion. When he is successful at this interim level expand the criterion again, until the student has reached the terminal objective. In this manner a student's successive approximations to the terminal goal can be reinforced and strengthened.

GUIDELINE 7

Punishment is defined as an event which, delivered contingent on a behavior, will decrease the probability of its occurrence.

Punishment refers to an aversive event that is delivered contingent on a response with a subsequent reduction in responding; that is, being reprimanded after hitting another child, writing "I was an exasperating, irritating child" one hundred times, or losing gym time. These all appear to be punishments —aversive events—and may have the same immediate effect: a reduction in behavior that led to the punishment.

It should be reiterated that these aversive events *might* lead to a reduction in response rate. Given the empirical rather than the dictionary definitions, it is possible to mistreat a child for talking—even beat him, for example—but if the beatings served to increase the amount of talking, the mistreatment would be defined as a positive reinforcer. There are several examples in the educational and psychological literature (Thomas, Becker, and Armstrong, 1968) when a teacher, trying to get a class to be quiet, tripled the number of reprimands. The class only became noisier. What probably happens in cases like this is that the child learns that he must be "bad" in order to get teacher attention, or that the punishment is worth the increased respect he gets from his peers, or the satisfaction he derives from living up to his own ideal image. What actually happens is more important than what a teacher thinks *ought* to happen.

Punishment or aversive consequences for behavior, when used precisely and carefully, can have immediate, short-term effects on behavior. Long-term effects have as yet not been adequately investigated, and it is suggested that punishment, if used at all, should be used judiciously. Preferably, punishment should be used only after a group of persons has reviewed the situation and finds it to be the only effective way of helping a child, and when it is felt that punishment will eliminate a behavior that produces even greater punishments for the child.

Although a great deal more research needs to be done in the area of punishment, it appears as if there are substantial risks involved in using punishment. Sometimes the use of punishment procedures, particularly if the effects are not monitored by observation, leads to the child attacking you or others in the environment. Sometimes this attack is direct, as an assault on a teacher; sometimes it is indirect, as destroying school property. When a person anticipates punishment he might also seek to avoid the punishment, and the child will very likely truant or avoid any contact with the punishing agent. In addition, the teacher might acquire aversive properties, and a genuine dislike for the teacher may result, which can limit the effectiveness of the teacher either as a role model or as a source of positive reinforcement. It is also quite possible that the student will model or imitate the punisher's behavior. Last, but by no means least, is the fact that punishment can be used to weaken a behavior in one setting, but that same behavior will occur with greater frequency and more intensity in other settings.

Most educators recognize that punishment, of one sort or another, is commonly used in all our school systems. At the same time there is also a growing body of literature which indicates that when punishment is used with precision and care it can be a valuable tool for the teacher in the classroom. As such the following guidelines for using punishment procedures should be of assistance.

1. Punishment should be administered consistently and contingent on the behavior you desire to decelerate. That is, do not deliver a punishment an hour after the child has behaved "poorly"—it should be done immediately so that the child is aware of the cause of the punishment and can adjust his behavior patterns.
2. Punishment should be administered without any undue demonstration of affect on your part. A demonstration of negative affect—rage, anger, hysteria—will probably be counterproductive. The child will pick up on your emotional state and will have learned an effective technique for controlling it.

3. There is some indication that reprimands that are delivered publicly and loudly tend to aggravate the problem and lead to further incidents of obstreperous behavior. The preferable technique is to deliver the reprimand softly and privately so as to allow the child to "save face" in class and to short-circuit any emotional reaction that might occur after a public reprimand. Such a technique has been found to be effective in decreasing obstreperous behavior (O'Leary and Becker, 1969).

4. The use of physical punishment is acceptable only under very limited conditions. It is necessary to have the consent and approval of parent and administrator prior to using physical punishment. Those cases in which physical punishment is to be used should be delineated for these authority figures in advance and should be based on an empirical criterion. The use of physical punishment is to be sanctioned only when the child is inflicting serious punishment on others. Aggression directed to others is a severe problem that might require a powerful solution such as physical punishment. But it must be recognized that such a procedure is not to be used indiscriminately.

5. The effects of punishment must be monitored by careful observation techniques to determine the effectiveness of your technique because, as indicated previously, presenting an aversive event may not decelerate the behavior but could instead cause other undesirable behavior.

Time Out An alternative to the punishment contingency is *time out*. Time out is that period of time during which the student is not able to earn reinforcers. A student is put into such a time-out phase after emitting specified inappropriate behaviors. There are several different time-out procedures you can use. In each case the behavior on which time out is contingent must be specified beforehand. For example, "Fighting will be followed by ten minutes of time out."

1. The ideal method for using time out is to segregate the student from the remainder of the class for the specified period of time. During that time the student receives no reinforcement and cannot interact with other students. He is allowed to return to the class when he has been quiet for the specified period. If he has not, if he has been raucous, then the time out is extended until that point when he meets specifications.

Although this situation is usually not achievable in the public school system, the following alternative is available.

2. The student remains in his seat for the time-out period but is not allowed to receive reinforcement of any kind for the duration of the time out. Other students in the class are informed that they are to ignore the student entering time out. The time-out student is informed of the time he will again be able to receive reinforcement. This should be contingent on appropriate behavior during the time-out phase.

At this point it is necessary to remember the consideration about using punishments, given above. A punishment may lead to aggressive and emotional behavior that may be worse than the behavior you were trying to avoid. It has been the authors' experience that in some school settings time out may be an extremely difficult situation to maintain. You may find that the child refuses to go into time out and thereby disrupts the class, or he may sit in his seat in a time-out period and annoy his neighbors. In any case it is wise to heed the advice given above. If punishment is going to be used, give it time to work. Just as we cannot expect extinction procedures to have an immediate effect, so we cannot expect punishment procedures to work immediately. Learning takes time.

We have repeatedly made reference to the use of reinforcers in behavior modification systems. One class of reinforcers is a learned reinforcer and is an integral part of almost all behavior modification systems.

GUIDELINE 8

A conditioned reinforcer is an event or object that has acquired its reinforcing properties through association with other reinforcers. There are several types of reinforcers. Primary reinforcers, such as food and warmth, require no previous learning to make them reinforcing. For a one-year-old child food and warmth can function as reinforcers. Points, stars, and tokens do not inherently function as reinforcers; the child must be conditioned to their use. This conditioning process is undertaken by simultaneously pairing the tokens, points, or stars with the primary reinforcer such as food. The same pairing process can be accomplished with a more generalized phenomenon such as teacher approval or praise. After they have been repeatedly paired together the praise, tokens, or points will function as conditioned reinforcers. Many teachers have found that just the simple act of increasing their own praise responses, and making them contingent on appropriate child behaviors has resulted in dramatic gains in achievement. When tokens or points are used in conjunction with praise the child soon learns that the points can have additional value, as they can be traded in for things with reinforcing properties such as food, games, choice of activities, and more tangible rewards.

Tokens have several advantages over the use of praise alone, and an analogy can be made between the use of tokens and money. Money, in and of itself, has no inherent value, but through its culturally determined buying power it has a great deal of worth to most people. Some of the more important reasons for the use of tokens are that they can bridge the delay between the response you wish to strengthen and the backup reinforcement that a child wishes to earn. In addition the use of tokens permits the reinforcement of almost any response at almost any time. It would not be desirable to interrupt a writing lesson and dispense Cokes, but it will not take more than a few seconds to distribute a token. Tokens can also be used to maintain performance over extended periods of time when the backup reinforcer cannot be distributed. Some researchers have also claimed that tokens may take on greater incentive value than a single primary reinforcer since the effects resulting from association with each primary reinforcer may be additive. Other advantages of using conditioned reinforcers are the fact that the teacher can provide the same reinforcement for individuals who have different preferences for backup reinforcers and, in addition, tokens are less subject to satiation states. A satiation state occurs when the individual has received such a surfeit of a reinforcer that it no longer has any reinforcing value and in fact may acquire noxious properties. An example of this occurs with food. A little bit of cherry pie is delicious to many people. But too much pie in one sitting is noxious, and a satiated person will try to avoid more contact with the cherry pie.

In summary, some of the definitions of reinforcement theory, principles, and procedures that are important in implementing programs are:

Guideline 1
A reinforcer is defined by its ability to accelerate, or increase, the rate at which a behavior will occur.

Guideline 2
The most advantageous time for dispensing reinforcers is immediately after the desired behavior is emitted.

Guideline 3
Extinction: A behavior that is not followed by reinforcement will decrease, or decelerate, in frequency.

Guideline 4
Be consistent and systematic. This principle applies not only to the administration of reinforcers but to the management of all behavior modification programs.

Guideline 5
Be specific in defining the dimensions of each reinforcer for your students.

Guideline 6
When a desired terminal behavior or the duration of that desired behavior is not currently attainable, then reinforcing successive approximations to that desired terminal behavior will eventually lead to the same result.

Guideline 7
Punishment or aversive consequences of behavior, when used precisely and carefully can have immediate, short-term effects on behavior.

Guideline 8
A conditioned reinforcer is an event or object that has acquired its reinforcing properties through association with other reinforcers.

REVIEW QUESTIONS

1. Upon entering the classroom, the teacher, Mrs. R., overheard Carol telling Judi, "My mother said that if I do all my homework for a whole week I can come to your house for the weekend." Was Carol's mother following guidelines delineated in this chapter or not? Explain your answer.

2. A point chart was taped to the front of the class and the teacher was distributing reinforcers to the students in the class. She was telling Vivian, one of the students in the class, "You can have your doll for five minutes but afterwards I want you to finish your lesson." What was wrong about this interaction and what do you think Vivian learned from it?

3. As the principal entered the classroom he noticed Benny messing up the book shelf, and heard the teacher yelling at him. When the principal later spoke with the teacher what advice do you think he gave her?

4. Donna told her mother that Mrs. Green, her teacher, yelled at her today after she had interrupted the reading lesson. Donna complained that Mrs. Green had never yelled before and that she was acting differently in class now. Which of the guidelines was the teacher not following through on and what could have been the result if she had followed the guideline?

5. "Sometimes I feel like hitting him, but I know that won't do any good." Is the inference here correct or incorrect and why?

6. A mother was overheard telling the teacher, "I want my son to do all his work in class and to do well. I know he's no angel and he's done poorly in the past but I want things to be different now." If you were the teacher which guideline(s) would you make use of in this case and what would you tell the mother?

7. "I always give the children in my class candy and toys and free time whenever they want it but they don't improve." Why might this intervention not be effective?

8. List five conditioned reinforcers that you could use in your class and five backup reinforcers that are cost-free.

9. What are the precautions that a teacher should take prior to using punishment as a behavior modification technique?

10. "The toys will be over by the door for anyone who wants them." What are some of the faults with this method of notifying the class about the distribution of reinforcers?

Chapter 2

The Token Economy

This chapter describes how to implement some of the principles and procedures of reinforcement systems into an ongoing classroom. The discussion focuses on the establishment of one type of classroom system called the token economy, the principles of which were explained in Chapter 1. In this chapter we describe the working and mechanics of a token economy. This system has been successfully used in numerous educational settings such as rural and urban elementary and secondary schools, special education classes, preschool and after-school centers, and in home settings as well.

A token economy is a motivation system based on exchanges in which the pupil, in exchange for emitting particular behaviors, receives or, more precisely, earns tokens or points; then tokens are in turn exchanged for something the pupil wants, such as free time, additional work, or access to games or teacher time. There is a contingent relationship between the behavior of the student (for example, reading behavior, specific acts of cooperation, writing, hand raising, and so on) and the tokens earned. The tokens are exchanged for activities, called *backup* reinforcers, so named because they essentially back up the token much as gold, theoretically, backs up paper money. Tokens usually function in accord with the principles of all other reinforcers; they differ primarily in that they are more manipulative. There are also other advantages in the use of tokens, as pointed out below.

In addition to the benefits already mentioned, tokens can bear a simple quantitative relation to the amount of reinforcement. Also tokens are portable; thus they can be awarded to the child in a number of settings such as on the playground, in the hall, at the easel, and elsewhere. Tokens are also a visible record of achievement which can lead to a facilitation of social reinforcement on the part of the teaching staff. Of equal importance is the fact that the tokens are later exchanged for a wide variety of backup reinforcers. Thus the teacher can take advantage of a variety of wants that exist for each student in the class.

Token systems appear to be fairly simple to manage. A child does his work, and is given a star for it. This star is then traded in for a piece of candy or for being the milk monitor. However, what appears at first glance to be so simple is really considerably more complex in its initiation and maintenance. Many teachers give stars and points or candy to their students. More frequently than not, after some success because of novelty, these systems fail. They do not fail because the general system is poor, but because the teachers did not apply some fundamental knowledge necessary to establish and maintain such a system. Giving children stars or candy or a pat on the back is usually not sufficient to motivate consistent new behavior or even to maintain present behavior. To use a token system successfully the teacher must identify the behaviors to be altered in such a way that they are objective and measurable, and in so clear-cut a fashion that both the child and the teacher will know when changes have occurred. The ability to apply the tokens in a specific time relationship with the behavior, the ability to find reinforcers that will have an effect on the behavior, and the use of adequate curriculum and teaching sequences are all necessary components of token systems.

Each of these three is a factor in reinforcement systems, but none can make the system work without the other two.

A token economy is dependent on establishing the tokens, points, or stars as conditioned reinforcers. Guideline 8 states that a conditioned reinforcer is an event or object that has acquired its reinforcing properties through association with other reinforcers. Through the simultaneous pairing of the token with a primary reinforcer such as food or warmth, or through teaching the child that a token can be exchanged for something of value, the token will begin to take on reinforcing properties. When this happens the tokens can be used quite effectively in strengthening and shaping behavior.

A step-by-step program for initiating a prototype of a token economy into your educational system follows. Programs similar to this one have been successfully implemented in several public schools throughout the country. As this program is described generally, it will have to be altered somewhat for each idiosyncratic environment in which it is placed. It does, however, present an overall plan for structuring your own systems.

WHAT BEHAVIORS DO YOU REINFORCE?

There are no a priori answers to the question: What behaviors do you reinforce? Your target objectives are whatever behaviors you want your students to engage in. Some teachers, hopefully very few, may want students to sit in a chair and work for the entire day; others may want students to volunteer answers more often; others may wish students to work in groups without fighting and disruption; and some teachers may want students to be able to move about the room without disturbing classmates. Regardless of which example fits your needs, after you select your target behaviors reinforce approximations to that target. This book cannot outline recipes for each program. Your sensitivity and expectations from your students at any given time will enable you to reinforce behaviors en route to the terminal objective. Below is an extensively detailed example of reinforcing successive approximations to the terminal objective of having a third grader work for an entire day in the class.

This case is admittedly extreme. It concerns a child with a long history of truancy and antisocial behavior. Most teachers will not have pupils with whom they will have to concentrate so hard on encouraging attendance and rudimentary skills, but the case does illustrate how academic skills were taught too. There were many reasons for the child's recalcitrant behavior, but his teacher was powerless to change the past and could only change his present environment so he would both learn in school and enjoy his school experiences as well.

> *Case 1.* Edwin refused to enter the room at the beginning of the year for any period of time longer than 5 minutes. Instead he would play in the halls. He would enter the room in the morning, hang up his coat, take a walk around the room, and leave for the rest of the day. A program was instituted for Edwin that reinforced approximations to our objectives of having him learn basic skills.
>
> 1. Initially, the teacher selected a behavior that the teacher wanted to encourage, and when Edwin engaged in the behavior it was reinforced. Thus, when Edwin entered the room to hang up his coat, the teacher gave him an M&M and told him that she was glad to see him in class and that he was getting one point for coming in so promptly. The first period of the day was to be a mathematics lesson, and the teacher had arranged to have Edwin's math material ready for him on his desk. The math material was designed by the teacher to be at his level, as determined by consultation with Edwin's teacher from the previous year. In this instance it was a series of 2-digit addition and subtraction problems that did not require exchanging.
>
> 2. If Edwin sat down he got another M&M and another point. If he began working on the math material he received an additional point. If he left the room he was ignored by the teacher.

3. When Edwin returned to the room, he was again reinforced. (The first approximation was to have Edwin in the room, and this was reinforced.) Again, the teacher had prepared the appropriate academic material for Edwin. If he reentered the room during reading period and sat down, he would have found either his reader open to a specified page with accompanying questions or else an SRA card and answer sheet on his desk. If he began working on the material he would also be immediately reinforced.

4. At the outset it was not expected that Edwin would stay in the room for any great length of time. A timer was used in this classroom and whenever the bell rang, if Edwin was *in the room*, regardless of what he was doing, he received points and an M&M, as did others in the class who were emitting target behaviors.

5. As Edwin remained in the room for longer periods of time, the requirements for reinforcement were changed and were made explicit to him. Now he was required to be seated or working when the bell went off; if he was working *or* seated, he received reinforcement; if he was playing, he did not receive reinforcement. The targeted behavior was now strictly related to academic performance. He was informed of the number of questions or pages in the text that had to be completed to be reinforced.

6. The length of time that Edwin was expected to remain seated or working was gradually extended from 1 minute to 45 minutes. Edwin's case was very special. He began to do his math for greater lengths of time but he would not be seated during this time. Instead, he would stand near his desk, lean over and work on his math material. Remember, at this point he was reinforced for being seated or working. As the criteria for reinforcement became longer, the magnitude of the reinforcement also became larger. Thus, he would receive ten points at the end of 10 or 15 minutes instead of one point. In this way he was not penalized for "being good."

7. If the criterion was raised and Edwin left the room or would not work, it indicated that the criteria were too high and had to be withdrawn and lowered to a level that he could achieve. After working at the lowered level and being reinforced, the criteria were raised again. (In this manner the student will always inform you of criteria that are too difficult to meet.) Edwin was eventually able to

work through the entire day with no major disruptions and without leaving the room. One occurrence of "leaving the room" was not sufficient to indicate that a change in criteria was necessary. There had to be several such occurrences that were unconnected to external factors—for example, nausea, or a fight before class.

In our final assessment of Edwin's academic and social development at the end of the year, many positive aspects were very evident and very reinforcing for us. Edwin began the year running through the hallways and not doing any academic work. Gradually, he began to remain in the classroom for longer periods of time and to begin working on reading and math work. When he entered the class he was reading *Come Along* (Houghton Mifflin)—a 2.1 grade level basal reader—and had difficulty with exchanging in addition and subtraction. Through the year, with the guidance provided by behavioral techniques, Edwin learned multiplication facts, was using Cuisenairre rods to multiply, divide, and fractionate, and was recognizing geometric shapes. At the end of the year he was beginning a 3.2 grade level basal reader—*More Roads To Follow* (Scott, Foresman) and had advanced on the SRA and Barnell-Loft reading material.

Throughout the year, Edwin's performance was being continually monitored on scoring sheets similar to those shown in Figure 1 (p. 35) and Figure 2 (p. 37).

Your students may present similar problems and through careful observation you will know when to alter your criteria for them. Test out your hunches and be aware of the necessity of avoiding reinforcing inappropriate behavior. Methods of handling specific problems such as what to do when only one child in class is disruptive, or how to reinforce only one child without arousing hostility from others, will be discussed in Chapter 3. Methods for handling special behavioral problems will also be discussed in that chapter.

THE EXCHANGE SYSTEM

You now know generally what, when, and how to reinforce your students. Let us now examine more closely how the exchange system itself works. First, be aware that the "prices" of the backup reinforcers do not remain constant throughout the program. At the beginning of the program, you will want every student to have enough points on the first day so that he can exchange them for reinforcers. This means two things: (1) You may wish to create many opportunities for earning points so that everyone will have a chance to get a backup reinforcer; and (2) you can either set the prices low enough so that everyone will get a reinforcer, or higher, depending on the amount of reinforcers you give out. It is important that on the first day, the student exchange his points for a backup reinforcer, thereby learning immediately how the system works.

Time Sequence

There are options for the length of time the token economy is to operate each day. You may think it is advisable to use the token economy for half a day or for one period a day, in the morning or in the afternoon. Whatever the time limit you set, the same basic principles and methods will apply. The program presented here is based on the full school day, incorporating activities that can be used for an entire class.

Points, Checks, and Stars

These reinforcers—points, checks, and stars—are grouped together because the same recording and distributing methods can be used for all three. Five general methods for recording and distributing these reinforcers are as follows:

1. *Teacher records points, checks, or stars for each student in public view of the group.* In this system a large chart listing each person's name is placed in a conspicuous place in the environment. Whenever the teacher gives a reinforcer, the check, star, or point is placed beside the individual's name. The teacher need not go to each individual desk to distribute reinforcers but can simply record them at a central location. Each student is able to locate his point totals in one part of the environment, and if he desires he may compare his

totals with those of his fellow classmates. Sometimes this comparison leads to a competition which makes the token more valuable to the students. Totals are added up after each specified time period and after each exchange has been completed. Each day the student is able to view his new total after the previous transactions are completed.

2. *Teacher records reinforcers in public view, and the student copies the amount on his own score sheets.* This method has been found to be very successful with students who are not completely aware of the workings of the system and require additional instructions. In such a system the students are continually aware of the amount of reinforcement they have received during the day and also of the exchanges that take place. This system can also be used as a precursor to using the recording system mentioned in method 1. It is actually a combination of methods 1 and 2.

Each time the teacher gives out a reinforcer she says, "Beverly, five points for penmanship." The teacher records the five points on the chart in the room. As she does so, Beverly marks five points next to penmanship on the grid on her desk. In this manner the student is continually made aware that the system is always operating and that she is earning points within the system.

3. *Teacher records performance on students' grids.* A facsimile of such a grid is presented on page 37. There is no public announcement in this method. The teacher walks through the class with a pencil or a rubber stamper and simply gives out the reinforcers without any undue disruption of the class procedures. This is an extremely effective method to use while the students are doing individual work; it is especially effective when the teacher is not lecturing or reading to the entire class. This method is highly recommended for classes in which there is an open classroom-type structure. In this situation the student can carry his grid with him and the teacher can reinforce the child's behavior wherever he is, without disrupting the remainder of the class.

This system is perhaps the most efficient one to use

after your program has been in effect for a while. By that time students can be reinforced for guarding their own grids and not losing them. Loss of grids is the major disadvantage of this system and can be somewhat overcome by keeping a daily balance for each child. In that way the loss of a grid means loss of, at the most, one day's points. An addition to this system may be a tally of each person's points in public view. This has several advantages discussed previously.

4. *Teacher records academic and social behavior summaries.* The fourth system is an excellent method for use especially in those situations in which math or reading materials are used and for which a record of social behavior is also desired. A sheet (see Figure 1) is placed on each desk. The

FIGURE 1   Score Sheet for Points Earned

Period 1	*Period 2*
Number of problems solved correctly _____	Number of problems solved correctly _____
Social behavior _____	Social behavior _____
Period 3	*Period 4*
Number of problems solved correctly _____	Number of problems solved correctly _____
Social behavior _____	Social behavior _____
Period 5	*Period 6*
Number of problems solved correctly _____	Number of problems solved correctly _____
Social behavior _____	Social behavior _____
Period 7	*Period 8*
Number of problems solved correctly _____	Number of problems solved correctly _____
Social behavior _____	Social behavior _____

Each problem solved correctly is worth 1 point.
Each social check is worth 2 points.

contingencies are given at the bottom: each problem solved correctly is worth 1 point in the token system. These points are added up at the end of the period. Each social behavior check is worth 2 points. The point values are, of course, arbitrary and can be changed based on student behavior. This chart can also be used for reading materials such as SRA and Sullivan in which there are reading problems available, or for those materials that you construct yourself. For those subjects that do not lend themselves to such a division, you may arbitrarily set a point total for completion of academic work. In this manner, the entire day may be recorded on the student's sheet. Totals can be taken at the end of the day and the exchanges made.

5. *Student records own reinforcers, based on teacher instructions.* This method is most expedient in saving teacher time. It is impractical at the outset of the program, until you are sure that there will be no cheating. Since this system is based totally on student honesty, the lack of such a quality in your population may lead to inaccurate results. In addition, in the early stages of the program, a student may fall prey to peer pressure and neglect to record his reinforcers or may augment them for the same reason. It is advisable to institute use of this method after your program has been functioning for some time and you are confident of your students' competence and reliability.

Each student has a small mimeographed grid taped to his or her desk (see Figure 2). When the teacher informs Joan of the number of points or stars she has received, Joan notes this on her grid. After a specified time Joan adds up her points and can exchange them for backup reinforcers, or save them. At the exchange, Joan's points can be subtracted by simply crossing them out.

The advantage of this system is that Joan knows how many points she has, and how many she needs for the backup reinforcers. It can be very reinforcing to Joan to write down the number of points she has received, and it can also be reinforcing for her to be aware that she has sole responsibility for recording her points.

NAME __Joan__ DATE __January 10, 1973__

CLASS __3–224__

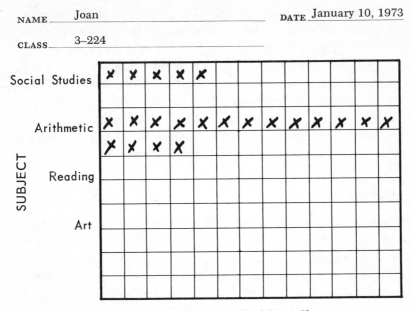

FIGURE 2   Reinforcement Grid Score Sheet

A disadvantage is that unless the reinforcers are distributed at the end of the period, there is liable to be some disruption due to a break in continuity.

By having the student score himself you can do away with some of your own bookkeeping, since the child's previous balance and current tally are on one sheet of paper. All you have to do is add the day's tally minus "purchases" to the previous balance. It is very simple, quick, and is easily understood by most children.

Regardless of which system you use, remember Guideline 4: Be consistent and systematic. If you are consistent and systematic, you will soon discover where the problems are and so will be able to remedy them.

It is also recommended that the teacher often include praise when administering these reinforcers. Ideally it should be done each time a student receives points. It is understood that this is quite difficult, but an effort should be made to praise the students as often as possible when they receive any conditioned reinforcers. In this way students will function as effectively under social reinforcement as token reinforcement.

Which of these five systems should be used will be determined by the kind of class you have and, at this point, only your own intuitive feeling for what will work best for your class. Probably in the course of the school year you will move from one system to the other. Facsimiles of scoring the recording sheets have been provided in Figures 1 and 2. You will find these helpful in designing your own system.

Trading Stamps

In this system each student has a booklet that is similar to a trading stamp book. The teacher or administrator of the reinforcers distributes trading stamps to the subjects in much the same way as is done with points and checks. Like one of the previous methods, the subject can carry his book with him and always be aware of his savings and earnings. The stamps are exchanged for backup reinforcers in the same manner as discussed above. At the designated exchange period the exchanged stamps are voided for the backup reinforcer. This system may be physically harder to manage than putting points on the board. It is advisable to distribute the stamps at the end of each academic period, which necessitates the use of this system only with those students who do not require immediate reinforcement.

Bogus Money

Fake money or play money, which can be made on ditto sheets, is distributed as reinforcers to the students, either during the lesson or at its conclusion. The money is exchanged at the specified time for backup reinforcement in the same manner as previously discussed.

Another method for using bogus money is to make the money yourself from cardboard or oaktag. The worldwide monetary systems all have portraits of famous individuals on their money. Whether you are a good artist or not you can "draw" pictures of your students on the various denominations. For example, a one point or dollar bill could have a drawing of José on it with his name in block letters: JOSÉ ONE DOLLAR BILL. Similarly, the ALICE FIVE DOLLAR BILL and the RAYMOND TEN DOLLAR BILL, and so forth. In addition to being good conditioned reinforcers they make good motivating materials for mathematics lessons. You may also want to make a child's appearance on a bill for one week as a possible backup reinforcer for a specified number of points.

Savings Books

Savings books are similar to bank books, into which credits for behaviors and academic work are entered. These may be exchanged for backup reinforcers.

Poker Chips

Another system consists of the distribution of poker chips or math counting blocks as conditioned reinforcers. Whenever the child produces the desired behavior a certain number of times, he is given the chip simultaneously with the social reinforcement. In several classrooms that have used these systems successfully the chip is placed in a cup which the youngster has on his desk. Younger children can wear aprons with pockets sewn in them. The advantage of the apron is that chips can be dispensed during activities when the youngster is not in his seat. Some teachers have also found it helpful to wear aprons so they can carry the tokens with them. In this system the recording can be minimal, but it requires effort to count out these chips when they are exchanged for the backups. One consideration to be aware of is that some students may rattle their chips and so provide extraneous and disruptive stimulation for the class.

In addition, chips can also be stolen. One of the most effective ways to deal with stealing is to make tokens in such a manner that they cannot be duplicated for any child that you suspect is stealing. In that way you can make sure that the child who steals has received his tokens only in the authorized manner, since he cannot trade in any tokens but those that have been denoted for him. Using a different colored chip is probably the easiest way to do this, but using a different shaped token or ones with distinguishing features such as holes punched in them will do as well.

Other recording systems and conditioned reinforcers can be used and depend on your own creativity. For example, a program has recently been devised that uses individual credit cards. Each student has an account file and makes deposits and withdrawals in much the same manner that business credit cards are used. Combinations of any of these systems can be used in any classroom. There is no one best method for every classroom.

Once you have decided on which system to use, you must learn how to apply it. This means you must be able to answer the question, *"When and how do I reinforce?"* The following suggestions should help you in using any of the systems discussed above.

1. Your physical, verbal, or facial attention will probably be reinforcing to your students. Give attention as often as possible and praise your students when deserved. Tell them how well they are doing and how pleased you are. There are positive aspects in every person's behavior and work. If you look for them you will find them, and when you do, praise them warmly.
2. Minimize the pointing out of negative aspects of behavior. Highlighting negative behaviors can reinforce them, and can increase the probability that they will recur. Statements such as, "Let's see if you can spend the day without getting into a fight" are actually "dares" that students will often take you up on. Rather than use statements that may elicit negative behaviors, maximize your opportunities to reinforce children positively. "You're doing great today," "beautiful work," "very good" are statements that can have great reinforcing effects on your students. Such verbal praise, administered as frequently as possible, can be important as a reinforcer.

Ordinarily you will have little or no trouble getting your token economy started, and getting your students to learn the principles at hand. However, for those of you who do experience such a problem the following suggestions are made.

How To Make Students Aware of the Principles of Reinforcement

At the outset of your program, points, stars, and checks will have few reinforcing properties of their own, so you must make them reinforcing. This is accomplished by pairing the conditioned reinforcers with teacher attention and praise *and* some backup reinforcer. It can be done in many ways.

1. With young children, kindergarten to fourth grade, you can dispense reinforcers when they enter the room and either hang up their clothes or sit at their desks or emit a behavior that you think is desirable. Give the students points as soon as they engage in appropriate behavior. While you distribute the points, praise the children. When they sit down you can give each student a small piece of candy in exchange for each point he has received. The candy should be quickly and easily consumable. M&Ms, mints, or pretzels are suitable for this purpose. Tell the students that they will be able to get prizes if they do their work and follow instructions, and what some of the prizes will be. Ask one student why he just received an M&M, what behavior did he have to emit? After this initial exchange arrange as many opportunities as possible for students to earn points and exchange them. Students must learn that earned points can be exchanged for any of the backup reinforcers that they can earn. Frequent exchanges at the outset of your program will help your students use the system.
2. Some students, especially in the lower grades, may have difficulty in discriminating the relationship of their behaviors to the available reinforcers. In such cases, you may wish to role-play the exchange, with the student taking the teacher's role, explaining the system, and rehearsing several interchanges. Other students may be disruptive until they see a friend receive a reinforcer, or until they themselves have received backup reinforcement. The more frequent the opportunity for earning conditioned reinforcers and exchanging

them for backup reinforcers, the quicker the students will adapt to the system.

3. Older students probably will not require as many interchanges to understand the exchange system. One rapid method of teaching them about exchange is to announce that the points they receive can be exchanged for money and other backup reinforcers. For example, "If you receive 10 points within the next hour you will be able to get five cents or a piece of gum. To earn 10 points you must complete the math lesson and the spelling work with 80 percent accuracy;" or, "To earn the nickel you must receive six checks in the next one-half hour. I will tell you when each 5-minute interval is finished. At that time, if you have been working, you will receive one check. At the end of a half hour, if you have been working all the time, you will have six checks and I will give you each a nickel." Such a contingency immediately makes points a valuable commodity, a reinforcer, and at the same time makes necessary and required behaviors quite explicit. This way only one message is being sent.

There is no reason why money must be used, although it is a very effective method. While at first it may appear to be foolproof, expect some negative reaction to this procedure from your students. Some may vociferously declare, "I don't want your Goddamn money or your Goddamn points." Such behavior should be extinguished by ignoring it, and at the same time continuing to reinforce those who are attending. There are few things harder for a teacher to do than to ignore consistent outbursts such as these. When your students observe that you do not "care" or attend to their negative behavior or that their friends are receiving money and other backup reinforcers, they will shortly begin to work to earn these same reinforcers. Once they are working within the system, you can exclude money from the backup reinforcer list or the reinforcing menu, discussed later in this chapter. You will probably receive some inquiry about this exclusion, but you can explain that money was only one reinforcer among many and that other reinforcers are available for their points. You might also promise that money may be used again in the future. You will probably think of other methods of introducing the reinforcement system, and of ways of helping students to understand the concept of exchange and the role of points and backup reinforcers within the system. *Let us point out again that you do not have to use money or consumable items to establish the relationship with older students.* You can use any social event that you feel is reinforcing, for example, 10 minutes free time, listening to records with earphones. We have discussed using money and other kinds of extrinsic reinforcement; this is sometimes advisable with special education classes that have special budgets, but it is by no means essential. There are many things that do not cost money, such as access to free time or listening to records.

It has been our experience with children in the lower grades that frequently when a contingency is stated for a large or an expensive reinforcer—use of the football, or a skateboard, or a free period—they get the impression that there is *only one* such reinforcer available. That is, they think that once the football is taken by someone, there will not be any more. This idea may be corrected by repeating that there are enough such reinforcers for everyone, or by stating the quantity of such reinforcers that are actually available. In the money contingency discussed earlier it was important that the students know that everyone who gets the six checks will get a nickel. Similarly, "Everyone will be allowed to paint for 10 minutes," or "Everyone will get a chance to be a monitor."

Counting Making someone aware of the frequency of an inappropriate behavior often has the effect of decelerating it. Making an adult aware of the fact that he picks his nose tends to reduce the frequency of that behavior in your presence, although it is not totally extinguished. Making a student aware of the number of times he emits an inappropriate behavior such as yelling, or the amount of time spent on such a behavior, often similarly reduces the frequency of the behavior. The method of tracking such behaviors is very simple: (1) Purchase a golf log wristband (two or three dollars) and wear it as a watch. The golf log is used by golfers to count the number of strokes they take in a game. The log can count to 99. It is usually used to record the behavior of only one student at a time. (2) Note the time you begin observing. (3) Whenever you observe the target behavior count it on your golf log. This involves no interruption in the flow of the lesson. (4) At the end of the day inform the student of the count or frequency of the behavior. (5) Repeat this procedure each day. (6) Note the time you complete each observation. The same technique can be used with a stopwatch, clocking the duration of a particular behavior. Simply being made aware of the counted time will often help a child decelerate the behavior. You should always use this technique in conjunction with some type of reinforcement program for accelerating the appropriate behaviors required. In this way reinforcement can be contingent on a reduction of the count. The student can count along with you, and be aware of his progress.

When Are Reinforcements Administered?

Several alternatives are available for the timing of administering reinforcements.

Using a Kitchen Timer Purchase a regular kitchen timer (two to six dollars) with a 60-minute sweep hand that can be set to the nearest minute. The timer is used as a signal mechanism for both you and your students. Set the timer to ring after a specified interval has elapsed. When this occurs you or your aide quickly observe which students are doing their work and which are not. In classes with many students you and your aide should decide which children each of you will observe—for example, you can observe the students on the right side of the room, and your aide can observe the remainder of the class. In this manner the whole class can be covered in a very short time. If you administer the points, your aide will inform you as to which students earned points. If your aide administers the points, saving you time, you then tell her which students in your group get points.

The key to this process is to be sure that the students

are unaware of when the bell will ring. If they receive points when the bell rings they must be constantly on the alert for it. This necessitates their attending all of the time, since they cannot be sure when it will ring. This is an excellent technique to use at the outset of any program, when students need constant monitoring and reminding of what they are to do.

How the timer is set involves sensitivity on your part as to how well the students are doing. With a disruptive class, it may be necessary to set it for very short intervals so that the students can receive a lot of reinforcement. Usually when the bell rings the students will make an effort to show you that they were working during the preceding interval. Be sure to reinforce only those children who were working. As the system continues you will be able to lengthen the timer intervals without risking disruptions. Eventually, the intervals will become long enough to administer reinforcers only at the end of each academic lesson and then at the end of each day.

There are three rules for using the timer: (1) At the outset of the program, set the time at short intervals and extend these at the students' pace; do not rush. (2) If the timer does not appear to be effective, set it manually and walk with it, so you can ring it when appropriate behavior is being emitted. Remember to associate verbal praise with the reinforcers that you administer. (3) Should you notice that the timer is no longer effective, stop using it. Your students may be telling you that they no longer require it, or that you must switch to a different technique.

Random Intervals Tokens can be distributed at any time during academic periods. If you do not wish to use the timer, there are several other alternatives. You may walk through the class during the lesson and at random intervals give out checks or stars. This system requires that you or your aide move about the room frequently. If you habitually stand in front of the room, your first step to walk around to distribute checks will signal the students that reinforcement is forthcoming. This signal will alert them to get into "studying position." You must state the requirements for reinforcement specifically: "You must be in your seat, working on the material during the entire interval, not just when I give out checks." Be certain that you are observing all of your students and that each one has an equal opportunity to receive reinforcement. Be aware of the criterion for reinforcement for each student. Do not spend all your time on one side of the room. Use your aide to assist in administering reinforcers.

Fixed Intervals Tokens can be distributed after the academic period is completed or after a fixed work period has elapsed. With students who demonstrate the ability to work for an entire period, you will be able to use fixed intervals of reinforcement. Tell your students that those who work for the entire time period will receive 10 points at the end of the period. The point total is chosen to approximate the average number of points they would have received had the reinforcement been given throughout the period. Similarly, those who worked only part of the time can receive a fractional amount of reinforcement. This method is extremely effective and will probably be set up as a goal for many systems. Not only does it inform the students of the requirements for reinforcement, it also eliminates disruptions that may occur while reinforcement is administered during the lesson. The timer can again be used here to denote the interval of time you are counting.

Mixed Intervals Use all three techniques at the same time. Inform the students that they may get points randomly, or at fixed intervals, or when the bell rings.

Fixed Ratio It can be made explicit to students that they will receive points only for correct answers given or words written or whatever specific criteria you set. At the beginning it is usually best to give one point for each correct answer given. This is the fastest way to build the behavior you want to develop. After this system has been in operation for a while you can give the same number of points for every two examples correct, and then every five examples, until you can begin to phase out of the token system entirely. The ratio should always be made explicit to the pupils.

The fixed ratio schedule is probably the easiest to use and most applicable with curriculum materials that have been artificially divided for you. (See Figure 1 for an example of a recording instrument for this system.) For example, each math problem correctly answered is exchanged for one point; each frame of the Sullivan Programmed readers or each question on the SRA cards can be exchanged for one point. If you do not use materials such as these or those listed in Chapter 5, then you can divide the material artificially. After reading the appropriate section in the basal reader, the student can be given a series of questions to answer. Each correct answer is exchanged for one point.

The system you decide to use should be determined by the behavior of your students. Familiarity with the examples above should help you to design this phase of your program.

The Reinforcement Menu

The menu is a list of reinforcers and their exchange value. You should place the menu where everyone will be able to see it. It should contain enough items for each child to purchase those he desires. Our experience has been that eight items is an absolute minimum. You may alter the items or their value whenever it is necessary. An example of a reinforcing menu follows.

Doll corner	10 tokens
Blocks	10 tokens
Puzzles	7 tokens
Library corner	7 tokens
Filmstrip projector and cartoons	15 tokens
Use of games	5 tokens
Drawing on chalkboard	3 tokens
Use of easel	3 tokens
Play with hamsters	5 tokens
Any item not on the menu	? tokens (to be discussed with your teacher)

In the menu above, the prices have been preset for didactic purposes only. In practice it is usually better to preset the prices and then announce them to the class. It is best to do so because often there is a tendency to set the prices according to how many tokens the students have, and in that way it is more likely that you will lower your standards to how much the students have actually accomplished rather than having the students meet your criteria. There is also the temptation to feel sorry for a student who does not have many tokens and therefore to adjust your prices accordingly. This does not help the student to grow in achievement.

The Display Case

One way to make the reinforcers more powerful is to display them. Place one sample of each backup reinforcer on a shelf or in a see-through bag or container so that it is always visible to the students. Those items that cannot be displayed in such a manner should be referred to verbally or in pictures. The display case is much like an advertisement for the program—it reminds the students that they can acquire these objects if they do their work.

It is crucial that your students be made aware of all the reinforcers available to them. As discussed previously, one reinforcer may be adequate for a short period of time, but for long periods and long programs you will need a larger selection. We cannot stress sufficiently how idiosyncratic reinforcers can be. Some people will travel miles to see a play and go at great sacrifice, whereas others would never consider spending an evening at the theater and would give away tickets to the same play. To some children games are reinforcing, but many children much prefer books. Always take into account the wide variety of tastes you are bound to find in your class and offer a wide variety of backups.

Choose any method you wish to review the reinforcers with your students. Be sure to do it whenever it is time for distributing backup reinforcers. You will find yourself altering the point values of the reinforcers as the program progresses. When this is done, you must make the students aware of it immediately, so that you do not get complaints later in the day about the change. Once the values are changed, the student will alter his own preferences to fit his own earnings and potential earnings.

HOW DO YOU ARRANGE THE EXCHANGE VALUES?

After locating your reinforcers, the price affixed to each will primarily be determined by whether or not it has monetary value, accessibility, and student preference.

Monetary Value

Candy bars will ultimately be your cheapest consumable reinforcer (approximately ten cents). A basketball, on the other hand, may cost you five dollars. You do not want one day's point accumulation (e.g., 50 points) to be able to be exchanged for a basketball. Initially, you do not want the student to have to save for four or five days for a candy bar. You must strike a compromise. First, estimate the probable number of points a person will be able to earn in one day if he does all of his work. If 30 points is the maximum, you are bound to have a majority of students earning less—for example, 22 to 25 points. Since you want everyone to be able to select a reinforcer at the end of the first day, or at least to know it can be acquired, you will have to set your exchange rates accordingly. Take 20 points as the base—your first approximation will be: one ten-cent candy bar is exchangeable for 20 points. In this case you may set a point-price ratio of 2 points equals one cent. In this manner a five-dollar basketball will cost 1000 points. You can follow this ratio for all items in between—a one-dollar yo-yo is exchangeable for 200 points; a 30-cent slice of pizza is exchangeable for 60 points; a 25-cent notebook is exchangeable for 50 points.

After this ratio has been functioning for several days, you may notice that everyone is earning between 25 and 30 points. That is, the students are working more and are able to earn the reinforcers with greater ease. When this occurs, raise your ratios and prices. You may raise them to 3 points exchangeable for one cent or 2½ points exchangeable for one cent, in which case your prices become 1500 points for the basketball and 30 points for the candy. The result of this modification is that it takes more points to get the reinforcers now than it did in the beginning. As your students become better workers you may raise the ratio to 10 points, exchangeable for one cent or as high as you can make it. If you have raised it too high, your students will inform you through their actions. If your backups are not functioning properly, lower the ratio to a more suitable level.

Make all of your changes in prices and ratios explicit to your students, but do not get trapped into bargaining or negotiating with them on how much each item on your menu is worth. It should be clearly understood that some items are cheaper than others, and that each child can select his own item on the menu if he has sufficient points. It is best not to get into the position of using points coercively or as bargaining points or as veiled threats. Students who are more adept at bargaining than at producing correct answers to math problems need much more practice with the latter task, and you can best help them by putting the former behavior on an extinction schedule.

You may find that certain items are very desirable and that most students are exchanging their points for that item—in the spring, water guns and baseball cards are very desirable and, as stated previously, in cold climates, during the winter, gloves are major reinforcers. When such situations develop take advantage of them by raising the point-price ratio for that item only. When the reinforcer is highly coveted you can make it contingent on a greater number of points and therefore a greater amount of work. Similarly, you may find that students no longer wish to consume an item at a high price. In that case, they can shift to a new item or you could reduce the price. Whatever your decision, be aware of its possible results.

This discussion has focused mainly on *monetary-valued reinforcers. We have not attended to social reinforcers that must be an integral part of any reinforcement menu.* We have included a list of socially oriented reinforcers in Chapter 1, page 8. In addition we have added an extensive list of social reinforcers that can be used in almost all classrooms (see Appendix A).

How do you assign point values to those reinforcers that have no monetary value?

Student Preference and Accessibility

You will have to estimate the worth of items that do not have monetary values (a walk in the hall, an extra music period, a visit with a favorite teacher). Reevaluate the worth of such activities after you observe the results in terms of student selection of that reinforcer. It cannot be emphasized enough that what teachers think is reinforcing for a child often is not the same as what the child finds reinforcing; only the child can determine what is an effective reinforcer for himself. The prices should be set in terms of its accessibility and student preference. The greater the desirability of the reinforcer, the higher the value. If everyone wants to take a walk in the hall, you must place a higher premium and therefore a higher exchange value on it so that it competes with all other reinforcers on an equal level. By raising the price of finger paints and keeping the price of regular paint at the same level, the finger paints will be bought only by those students who are willing to forego other purchases. Thus, by increasing the value of the walk in the hall you weed out those students for whom this is not as desirable as another item worth the same amount. Following the rules for reinforcers, the students should be aware of the time and place during the day that these reinforcers can be enjoyed.

Accessibility to the reinforcer must be accounted for. For example, there are specific times during the day when these reinforcers are available. The shorter the time of their availability, the fewer the opportunities, the greater the point value. Whatever your initial exchange values are, be prepared to alter them when the situation arises. Be ready to raise or lower the point-price ratio as it becomes necessary, within the guidelines mentioned above.

Another technique is to let students "buy out" of activities such as music or gym if the student finds these activities distasteful. It has been noted that having students work harder at basic skills to avoid less vital skills, at least temporarily, can be a powerful aid to a token system.

MAINTAINING THE SYSTEM

As your program progresses you will have other decisions to make. Although token systems that have been put into operation are remarkably successful, some teachers have trouble getting their programs started for the following three reasons: (1) *The teacher is failing to reinforce some students adequately;* (2) *students are given academic materials that are too hard for them and therefore they cannot make the appropriate responses;* and (3) *the backup reinforcers are of little value to the students, or are priced disproportionately for the amount of work required to earn them.*

During your program it would be most wise to refer to these three problem areas and to observe which, if any, are at work in your program. Check the students' materials and determine if they are contributing to disruptive behaviors; observe yourself or have your aide observe whether you are reinforcing all the students or tend to be biased toward some. You can also ask the students if they want any other items included on the reinforcement menu. We are not advising you to stop at a particular point in your program to do this, but rather to monitor the program throughout consistently.

PHASING OUT
REINFORCEMENT SYSTEMS

The ideal situation is to phase out the extrinsic reinforcement systems, like token economies, and to have the children responsive to social reinforcers and the curriculum per se. This can best be done through careful observation, and making certain that you have been pairing tokens, backup reinforcers, social praise, and primary reinforcers. We have been using tokens to build the foundations of the child's behavioral repertoire. Once this is established the behaviors will be able to be maintained by natural contingencies. However, this doesn't happen magically. There have been many arguments and techniques put forward to accomplish this objective. Several studies have found that the use of reinforcers that are natural to the school environment can easily be substituted for those backup reinforcers that are artificially part of the environment. Monitor jobs, special academic materials, and so forth, can be used as natural reinforcers, as has been suggested previously. The withdrawal of the artificial token system and the maintenance of appropriate behavior could then be accomplished using these natural reinforcers in association with your verbal and physical attention, which are themselves strong reinforcers.

The move to natural reinforcers such as praise and the content of the subject itself should always be done in conjunction with careful data analysis. The section describing how to take academic rate measures will be one of your most useful guides. If there is a drop in the student's output, that usually indicates that you have phased out of your system too quickly. Set up your token or contingency system again, and try to work out a different reinforcement schedule. In any case, your data will be the best guide to effectiveness.

The total withdrawal of tokens and points can be accomplished if you follow the directions given above. There are, however, other reinforcement systems you may wish to use in place of the token system. As we know, behavior is maintained by reinforcement; even if you don't have a token system in effect, *you must continue to reinforce the appropriate behaviors*. The following chapter presents several alternatives to token economies. These can serve as a substitute for the token economy, or as systems to use after you have withdrawn the token economy.

REVIEW QUESTIONS

1. List four strengths of a token system mentioned in this text and two potential problems.
2. What are some of the crucial ingredients of a token system according to this chapter?
3. In one class the teacher had children work on arithmetic in programmed texts. She then distributed the key so that the children could check their own answers. After checking their own work, they announced to the teacher how many examples they had gotten correct. She gave them one token for every problem that they said they had gotten correct. What is a potential problem in the situation?
4. In a token economy, what are some of the advantages to pre-setting prices and making them public?
5. What are two ways, mentioned in this chapter, of dealing with the stealing of tokens in a token economy?
6. Can you tell beforehand which reinforcers on a menu are going to be effective?
7. List three reasons mentioned in this text why token systems can fail.

Chapter 3

HISTORY

SPELLING

READING

ARITHMETIC

Alternatives to the Token Economy

There are some who object to using token economies for an entire group because of their worries about monetary commitment, although it must be pointed out again that there are many free reinforcers such as recess, games, monitor jobs, and so forth, available in school. Other objections are that there may be only one or two problem students in the class, or the recording system may be too complex, or there may not be adequate personnel to implement the system.

While the discussion of the token economy in Chapter 2 is fairly extensive and includes procedures for an entire class, there are single child applications of the token economy that are pertinent to specific problems in the classroom. In these systems the token economy, with its recording and exchange procedures, is directed toward one, two, or three children in the class. Frequently such applications are questioned from the standpoint of the effects such a program will have on the remainder of the class. These questions will be dealt with later in this chapter.

Case 2   A Single Child Application of the Token Economy
Anita was in a fifth grade class of 29 children. Of the entire class she was the only student with whom Mrs. O. was having trouble. She would stay in the room, but re-

fused to do any of the assigned work at her level. She consistently annoyed the others in the class by calling them names or yelling obscenities at them. Mrs. O. had ignored Anita's inappropriate behavior, but it continued. The teacher then decided to implement a single child token economy system, employing the class as her assistants. The following contingency was then arranged:

If Anita finished her assignment for the first period, she would receive 10 points. If she finished her assignment for the second period, she would receive an additional 10 points, and so forth. The points Anita earned were to be exchanged by the *class* for something the *class* could use, for example, a class pizza party, an extra recess period, or a trip. In this manner Anita was earning points for the entire class. The teacher then explained how the class could help Anita. They were to ignore all of Anita's outbursts and attention-seeking behaviors and respond to her only while she was attending to her work. When this occurred, her classmates could help her with her work, sit next to her, and encourage her to finish. During the following two-day period Anita continued to be obstreperous, and the class ignored her, being reminded to do so by Mrs. O. On the third day, Anita took out her book during the first period and was deluged with assistance from her classmates. First, Sue asked Mrs. O. if she could help Anita and was given permission. Then Ron helped her complete the first assignment. Although Anita did have occasional outbursts thereafter, she was now completing most of her work and improving in her social behaviors. By the following month, within 11 days, Anita had earned enough points for a class party. The next contingency was arranged so that it would take a longer period of time for Anita to earn the backup reinforcer.

While this technique can be effective, it is important to monitor it carefully. Sometimes peers will try to coerce a child into earning points, and negative as well as positive behavior can be reinforced. Because reinforcement is so powerful it must be used with extreme care.

In the case of Anita the teacher and class were following principles discussed in Chapter 1. Anita was reinforced contingent on appropriate behavior or approximations to it. Anita's inappropriate behavior was extinguished by the absence of attention from teacher and the students, and the reinforcement of compatible (socially appropriate) behavior. The students, in turn, were reinforced for cooperative behavior with a class party. The recording system used by the teacher was very simple and was managed by several of the students.

This type of reinforcement system can be used when you have only one, two, or three students to cope with. If you do not wish to spend money on reinforcers, you could set up similar contingencies using an extra free play period, or gym time, or a trip, as contingent backup reinforcers. (See list of potential backup reinforcers in Chapter 2 and in Appendix A.)

The use of this single child application with the *class sharing the reinforcer* may extricate you from a problem that can be encountered when one child receives reinforcement and the remainder of the class does not. In such a situation it would have been probable for other students to react inappropriately when they saw that only Anita was being reinforced. You can avoid that problem by having the whole class partake in the reinforcement.

There are other alternatives to the single child application of the token economy. One alternative is a contingency management system for the individuals involved or, for that matter, for each member of the class.

CONTINGENCY CONTRACTING

The contingency contract is very much like a business deal between two people—in this case, the student and the teacher. It is an IF-THEN statement regarding the behavior the teacher desires the student to emit and the reinforcement he receives for it. After observing the student and noting the behaviors that you wish to strengthen, you can arrange a contract with him, in essence an individual reinforcement menu, and together decide on the contract.

Case 3

Gregory was a third grader who had a great deal of trouble learning arithmetic skills. Mrs. R. was aware that Gregory wanted to visit her home after school. A contingency contract was then arranged: if Gregory did all his work in school for five consecutive days and learned how to do exchanges in subtraction, then Mrs. R. would take him to her home on the fifth day for one and one-half hours. Both agreed to the contract.

On the fourth day Gregory did no work. The contract was not observed, and Mrs. R. decided that the interval they had set was too long for Gregory. Gregory had been fine for three days, but evidently the behavior was not yet strong enough. Gregory could not take such a long interval without the backup reinforcement. The contract was renegotiated. Four days of successful work was now exchangeable for a trip to the teacher's home. Unlike the previous contract, this one was completed. Gregory did all his work and learned his subtraction skills. Consequently he was taken to Mrs. R.'s home. A new contract was then agreed on for five days of successful work including subtracting three-place numbers (e.g., 159 from 315). After some time new reinforcers were found for his academic behaviors which were then included within a new contingency contract. This follows our previous suggestions (page 52) regarding the maintenance of your program. By the end of the school year Gregory's contracts were based on several weeks of appropriate behavior prior to reinforcement.

Just as Mrs. R. moved with Gregory through several approximations to a target objective, you can arrange similar contingency contracts for each member of your class or for specific students within the class. The requirements for such contracts are (1) specified behavior, (2) specified duration of behavior, and (3) specified contingent reinforcers agreed on by both the teachers and the student. Be prepared to alter the first, second, or third elements of this contract when you notice the contract is not being fulfilled or has been successfully fulfilled. To simplify your task in arranging these contingencies, you can use a form similar to the one shown in Figure 3

CONTINGENCY CONTRACT

Student's Name _____	Teacher's Name _____									
1—IF: _____, does										
2—_____ (Behavior—specify amount and/or duration)										
3—THEN: _____										
Day or Lesson	1	2	3	4	5	6	7	8	9	10	Total
	Y	Y	Y	Y	Y	Y	Y	Y	Y	Y	
	N	N	N	N	N	N	N	N	N	N	

FIGURE 3

for each student behavior. After each day or specified time period (hour, half hour, half day) you are to record if that part of the contract was fulfilled. This is your recording system for each student's behavior. By filing such a card you will have a record of past contracts and of the reinforcers that have been used, and will be able to chart the progress each student has made.

THE CONTINGENCY CLASSROOM

Different events and academic subjects have greater or lesser attraction for each student. The arrangement of these events and academic periods into hierarchies of preference where the higher preference event is contingent on a lower preference event is called the contingency classroom. This system is self-enclosed in that *it makes no use of reinforcers that are extrinsic to the everyday classroom activities* and does not involve an expenditure of money. It does, however, call for a detailed examination of each student's preferences and abilities, and the ability on your part to program them properly and to be flexible enough to alter choices frequently.

Follow this program for implementing your system:

1. Observe your students carefully: (*a*) What are your students' academic preferences and dislikes? (*b*) What are their academic weaknesses and strengths? (*c*) Which individuals prefer to work in groups? (*d*) Which individuals prefer to work alone? (*e*) What is done by each student during free time? (*f*) Who are the leaders of the groups? (*g*) Who is able to arrange activities?
2. For each student, rank order academic preferences, from subjects in which he is most interested to those in which he is least interested.
3. For each student, rank order academic weaknesses and strengths.
4. List the answers for questions 1 *c* through *g*, above.
5. List those events that can occur during the school day that do not pertain to regular academic work or that you can add to the class day—for example, monitor jobs (specify them all), milk and cookies for lower grades, free time, extra art time, music time, group singing, working with a microscope, using a typewriter, remedial education from peers or teacher, acting, presenting puppet shows, or any other event that is available to you in the school that your students may want to use. Several such reinforcers have been listed previously. Others that you may wish to use are reading a story, private discussions with teacher, use of crayons in a coloring book, drawing on blackboard, and learning to write in script.
6. Based on your answer to the questions in item 1 above, make a daily lesson plan for each student in which higher preference subjects are contingent on lower preference subjects.

Figures 4 and 5 are examples of such lesson plans for two fourth graders. These plans are to be placed on the individual's desk at the beginning of each day.

Case 4

Terry and the remainder of the class began the day with math—though they each had different assignments. The second subject was contingent on "successful" completion of the lesson. "Successful" should be defined by you at the beginning of each lesson or assignment. [For Terry, it was 85 percent correct.] When the math lesson was completed and checked by the teacher and so noted on the stu-

NAME: Terry	Complete	Incomplete
(1) Math [pp. 38–40] 85% correct [45 min.]		
(2) Art [30 min.]		
(3) Reading [pp. 135–150] [with group] ques. 1–6 [45 min.]		
(4) Free time [40 min.]		
(5) Lunch		
(6) Composition [Title] [30 min.]		
(7) Board monitor [5 min.]		
(8) Science [30 min.] [in group]		
(9) Extra time with microscope [15 min.]		
(10) Maps [Navigation] [20 min.]		
(11) Gym [30 min.]		

FIGURE 4

dent's lesson plan, the students then advanced to the higher preference event—art or typewriting. The duration of the higher probability events must be specified. The students then progress through the remainder of the day alternating between high and low preference events. The last event, gym, is the highest preference event and is made contingent on completion of *all* the previous events. Those individuals who have not completed all the events must return to those subjects and correct them. When that is done they can participate in gym.

At the outset you will encounter problems in coordinating the activities of each student with those of the others, but this can be overcome when you discover how long it takes each student to complete a lesson in each subject area. For example, you may observe that it takes Terry 60 minutes to complete a math lesson—instead of the 45 minutes that had been assigned. This necessitates one of two revisions: reducing her

NAME: Ricky	Complete	Incomplete
(1) Math [pp. 1–5] 80% correct [45 min.]		
(2) Typewriter [30 min.]		
(3) Reading [pp. 135–150] [with group] ques. 1–6 [45 min.]		
(4) Help Albert with reading [40 min.] [pp. 14–20]		
(5) Lunch		
(6) Composition [Title] [30 min.]		
(7) Five-minute walk with pass		
(8) Science [30 min.] [in group]		
(9) Free time [15 min.]		
(10) Spelling—Lesson 17 [20 min.]		
(11) Gym [30 min.]		

FIGURE 5

art time by 15 minutes or reducing the amount of work necessary to get to the art period. The latter choice is the more advisable, as by successive approximations you will avoid moving more quickly than Terry can.

Since each high preference event is contingent on an academic subject, if a student decides that he does not want to complete that subject, then he cannot enter the next contingency event (e.g., free time). In the event that he disregards these rules and forces himself into the next event, you must set contingencies so that he will leave. The best way of doing this is to reinforce all those in the class who break off contact with that student or to ignore him when he makes contact. He should be told that he can still enter free time in the appropriate manner if he completes his work. The above extinction process may take many days to accomplish, but will succeed if you are consistent and do not give in. Do not under any circumstances allow the child to use any reinforcer such as games, access to the board for drawing, and so forth, *unless* these have been earned. While this system is operating, the principles of behavioral management enumerated in Chapter 1 remain in effect, and you should constantly use verbal praise for appropriate behaviors and ignore inappropriate behaviors.

This system works well with children in the upper grades, but may present some problems with students who need more constant and immediate reinforcement and with those who have histories of "hall-running." In the latter case, children leave the classroom, find someone in the hall to interact with, and do not return for long periods of time. In such cases you must consistently ignore the hall-running behavior, and be sure to have more exciting events happening in your classroom than in the halls. In these cases you will have to receive permission from the school administrator to leave a child unattended in the halls. It is most important that the administrator understand that this is one important part of an integrated method that you are using in your class. (In situations where there is a present danger in allowing students in the halls unattended, we advise you to take necessary measures to safeguard your student's welfare.)

When the student enters the classroom he is to enter the event programmed for that time, or the previous subject if he entered during the high preference event. Alternative solutions are to arrange a single child application of the token economy for that student, or to arrange a contingency contract with him for the specified behavior.

In the examples above each low preference event was followed by a high preference event. This sequence is necessary at the beginning of a program, but you should aim for its rearrangement. One of the goals to set for yourself is to have two, three, four, or even five low preference events chained together prior to the students being allowed to participate in any high probability event. You will be able to arrange such a situation when you notice that the students are able to move through each low preference event rapidly, with very little difficulty and with few disruptions. When this occurs you can begin to program two low preference events together followed by a high preference event, and later extend your chain to three, four, and five low preference events.

We have consistently made reference to academic subjects being of low preference. This is a relative term; you may have students who consider reading and math activities of higher preference than typing, free time, or art work. In such cases we are ahead of the game, and the programming problem is simplified. You can program several such activities together without worrying about contingent reinforcers between events, as the materials themselves are reinforcing the behaviors. Of course, when such a student sees the other children participating in games or free-time activities he may want to join. Contingencies can be simply arranged to accommodate such students.

The Open Contingency Classroom Using a Token Economy

In this system the students use the points they have earned for academic behaviors to enter other academic events in which they can earn a greater number of points.

Case 5

From the moment students enter the classroom they know they can earn points for any academic work and for any specified behaviors the teacher has programmed, for example, 5 extra points for helping a classmate with his work. The classroom is divided into areas—reading, math, science, social studies, and a play area. Within this class, Beverly knew that if she completed the reading assignment prepared for her she could receive 50 points. Beverly was also aware that she could receive 25 points for completing her science assignment. The payoffs had been arranged by the teacher to take account of each individual's strengths and weaknesses. Beverly was weak in phonics skills but was strong in science. Taking advantage of these facts, the teacher made entrance to the reading area, a skill that needed strengthening, a more attractive possibility by giving it a higher payoff. Beverly still had her choice between all areas and probably could have avoided reading for two or three days. The teacher is explicitly encouraging Beverly to enter the reading area. Once there, all the forces of differential reinforcement will combine to strengthen such behavior in the future.

The students must be informed that the payoffs will differ for each student and should be given the reason for such differences. This will eliminate many problems that may develop in this area in the future. When you begin to notice that the students are accumulating more points than they can spend, it is time to raise the entrance fees, or lower the payoffs, or provide additional backup reinforcers for them. Several such reinforcers are listed in the previous section.

Because of the lack of supervision in most of the areas, you may find that it is necessary to use a timer and reinforce the students for appropriate conduct within each area, and for attending to the time intervals and limits they are allowed within each area. Any student who attends to the timer and leaves when his time is up, or enters a new event at the appropriate time, should be given extra points. You can set higher premiums for areas that are unsupervised in contrast to areas that are supervised by you or an aide at the time the timer rings. All recording systems discussed in the previous chapter can be used here. One or two students who have earned a sufficient number of points can use a facsimile of a bank book in which points, payoffs, and backup reinforcers can be charted simply and without taking up much time. That is, these students give out the points and do all the exchanges while keeping track of timers and allowing you the freedom to move about the areas. This system is an integration of the contingency classroom and the token economy. Procedures and principles applicable to this system can be found in the previous discussions.

Extra School Backup
Reinforcement

A primary objective in one program that was begun in the public schools was to enlist the support and assistance of the parents of those children in our program. Parents control a wide range of home-based reinforcers over which a teacher would normally have little influence, and their integration within an overall reinforcement system would therefore be of immense help to you and your students.

The integration of backup reinforcers that are based outside of school within a token economy or contingency management system augments the diversity of your reinforcement program. Such integration tends to make the parents and the community more active and interested in their children's progress. The reinforcers to which we refer are those that are home-oriented and managed by the parents and those that occur after school in the local neighborhood. Watching TV, extra allowance, going to a movie, going to gym after school, having friends come to the house, sleeping at a friend's house, staying out extra late, and opportunities to increase vocational skills after school are all backup reinforcers that you can employ with some outside assistance. It is possible to make any of the outside backup reinforcers contingent on any school-based behavior by introducing them into one of the systems enumerated.

With older students the key to this system is to enlist outside assistance. Ask the students what they most want to do outside school during their free time. You may get requests for jobs dealing with increased mechanical skills, typing skills, dark room procedures, counterman skills, and so forth. It is possible that these jobs or apprenticeships for training can be made available to your students if you present the alternatives to the respective employers in your community. The employer might be willing to give the students some pay for helping out at the shop after school. In so doing, the student will also be receiving training for future work. Other advantages to such hiring practices can be presented to the employer, emphasizing the benefit to the community and the alternatives if the students do not acquire these skills. Of course, such opportunities can be made contingent on classroom attendance and work. In addition to such outside assistance, the cooperation of parents should be sought.

Parents are usually brought into the educational system when their children have been disruptive rather than when they have been constructive. Systems in which the parent is able to monitor the child's academic and social behavior in school each day can be beneficial to the classroom situation. Making parents aware of the daily behavior of their children, and having home-based reinforcers contingent on appropriate behavior, is an excellent system. Some parents of course will not be cooperative in this endeavor, but our experience is that most parents *are* looking for *concrete* ways to help their children. One such method is illustrated in the section that follows.

DAILY BEHAVIOR REPORT

You can fill out a Daily Behavior Report (see Figure 6) at the end of each day. Your comment on whether or not the student should receive his reinforcement for that day is to be noted for the parent. Classroom reinforcements can be made contingent on getting parental signatures each day.

Such a daily monitoring system has many advantages:

1. It makes the student aware that his parents are cognizant of his daily work, thus adding another maintenance stimulus.
2. It makes the parents aware of their children's school behavior.
3. It can be integrated within any of the systems described above, or be used as an independent system, as the only behavioral modification system in effect.

Before instituting such a system, you will have to acquaint the parents with its workings, in essence the principles outlined in Chapter 1.

Daily Behavior Report

Name				Class
Teacher				

Date	Behavior	Academic Work	Home Reinforcement	Parent Remarks
Jan. 2	A B C D F	A B C D F	Yes No	
3	A B C D F	A B C D F	Yes No	
4	A B C D F	A B C D F	Yes No	
5	A B C D F	A B C D F	Yes No	
8	A B C D F	A B C D F	Yes No	
9	A B C D F	A B C D F	Yes No	
10	A B C D F	A B C D F	Yes No	
11	A B C D F	A B C D F	Yes No	
12	A B C D F	A B C D F	Yes No	
•	A B C D F	A B C D F	Yes No	
•	A B C D F	A B C D F	Yes No	
•	A B C D F	A B C D F	Yes No	
•	A B C D F	A B C D F	Yes No	
•	A B C D F	A B C D F	Yes No	
•	A B C D F	A B C D F	Yes No	

Figure 6

Group Cohesiveness

Both aversive and positive peer reinforcements are potential maintainers of behavior in the classroom. You may find that some students will not respond to individual contingencies for reinforcement or may try to sabotage the system you have set up in the class. For these students group cohesiveness can be used as a behavior modification technique.

How to Encourage Group Cohesiveness Select a reinforcer in which the entire class can participate, for example, redecorating the class, or making a trip. Set the following contingency for this reinforcer: if everyone earns "enough" (specify) points, then everyone will be able to take part; if one or two students do not get enough points, then no one will. The following dynamics will probably manifest themselves in the classroom. The students will begin to monitor their own behavior as well as the behavior of their peers. Those students having difficulty academically or socially will receive guidance from their peers. In this system you must allow for movement of students within the class and consistent verbal interchanges between students to remind each other to attend. As pointed out before, in our discussion of Case 2, one danger of this system is that the students may use aversive control to get the remainder of the class to attend. That is, threats of punishment may emanate from such a system unless you control them. Techniques for such control are class-specific. They may entail reinforcing cooperation and assistance, or having individuals tutor other, slower students or difficult learners, and reinforcing both the teacher and learner for successful performance on their specific tasks. Also reinforce the social behavior of those children who help others. An interchange between children such as, "Sit down, Malvina, or you won't get your work done," is an example of the kind of peer assistance that should be reinforced—not, "Sit down, Malvina, or else!"

A very interesting and simple technique for using group pressure efficiently is called "the good-behavior game" (Barrish, Saunders, and Wolf, 1969). The class is divided in half (or thirds, if necessary). The following instructions are given: "The team that wins this game will receive certain privileges (which you enumerate). The team that follows the rules most consistently wins. The rules are: During the math period there is to be no one out of his seat and no talking without permission. If anyone on your team gets out of his seat or talks without permission that team will get 1 point on the board. The team with fewer than 5 points for the period wins. If there is a tie you all get the privilege." Privileges suggested by the authors of this game are: wearing victory tags, having a star placed next to each person's name, lining up first for lunch, taking part in an extra project. Any of the previously mentioned reinforcers can be substituted. This game can be used for any specified period or for the entire day. A possible alternative is to have the game in effect for the entire week, and have a supplementary reinforcer for the team that does best at the end of the week. Again, check your reinforcers frequently, and do not become overly dependent on any one technique. If you do not wish to set up a competitive system, you can award prizes to all of those that meet the criterion. Hopefully, everyone will win!

AUXILIARY SYSTEMS

Many systems can be used to maximize short-term guidance which may or may not be incorporated within a larger system.

1. Place a list in a conspicuous place in the room. Each time an individual leaves the room, fights, yells, curses, throws a chair, and so forth, or whenever an inappropriate behavior you have signified occurs, then that student gets a check or a mark next to his name indicating the occurrence. The student or students with the fewest number of such marks are to receive a bonus number of points for your token system, or some other reinforcement if you are employing a different system. The behaviors must, as always, be specified and as the class progresses, the criteria must be altered. For example, initially you may find that many students get only two checks a day. When this occurs, raise your criteria and state that those who get one check or none at all will be given an extra bonus. When you notice that more students are achieving these criteria, you may wish to drop the system altogether. In that event, if you notice an increase in inappropriate behavior, then it is time to institute once again this or some other system.

2. A reversal of this system can also be employed. Students may get checks, or other forms of recognition, for extra fine work: helping a friend with academic work, or volunteering for a difficult task, or breaking up a fight, and so forth. The individual with the greatest number of helping points each day receives a bonus number of points.

It is also possible to use both of these procedures simultaneously.

PRESCRIPTIONS FOR CHANGE

Cursing

The frequency of children cursing teachers in inner-city schools is very high. Cursing may be the only way a child, in a world of grown-ups, can strike back. Teachers and educators should therefore not take cursing as a personal attack deserving retaliation. One method of extinguishing cursing is to ignore it, completely. As with most extinction procedures, cursing will decrease in a slow pattern: it will not disappear in one or two days; it may take weeks of consistently ignoring that behavior. If you remain consistent, patient, and tolerant while the student is testing you, the behavior will extinguish. Cursing is most often reinforced by a teacher's reply or by a friend's endorsement. By ignoring the cursing behavior you are eliminating most of the reinforcement that is maintaining it. By reinforcing other students in the class for ignoring such behavior, that behavior will eventually be extinguished. Remember to reinforce the student for noninvective speech. We know cursing is difficult to ignore, but it can be extinguished if you go about it systematically.

Fighting

Fighting is a behavior that poses some danger in the lower grades and a greater amount of danger and trouble in the upper grades. There are several methods to cope with such eruptions.

Distinguish between fun fights and real fights. The former are most often maintained by a teacher's reaction to them. Knowing that the teacher will attend to such disruptions tends to increase their frequency. They should be ignored by you and the other students in the class. Real fights should be broken up immediately, and the children should be separated until they have calmed down and can resolve their differences.

When children are fun fighting or insulting each other these procedures may be effective:

1. When verbal abuse erupts tell the class to face you and to ignore those students who are sparring.
2. Reinforce all those children who are facing you with praise and points, if you are using them.
3. Without any unusual statement continue with the lesson and continue to disregard the sparrer.
4. When the antagonists return to their seats inform them of the nature of the lesson without comment on the previous outbursts. When they begin the lesson and do their work, praise them for working. This, of course, may not occur till quite a while after the fight has ended. Sulking, moping, and cursing may fill this interval before appropriate behavior is again evidenced.

This technique may seem difficult to follow through on, and may raise some eyebrows of fellow teachers and administrators, but it has been successful where other methods have failed. Those fights that are not attention-seeking and that pose a definite danger to the participants should certainly be interrupted by you or, if possible, by their peers, with your approval. The rules of your school are not to be superseded by these behavior modification techniques.

If you are managing a token economy, you may set up certain rules regarding fighting such as (1) those students who fight lose 50 points (this is effective only if the points have value to the student); (2) those students who ignore the ones who attempt to initiate a fight receive 50 points. The student who attempted to initiate the fight but was not successful is not penalized in this case, and if in fact he is ignored by the students and teacher he will be less likely to attempt to pick fights in the future. The reason for not penalizing the individual who unsuccessfully attempts to initiate a fight is that such behavior on your part will most likely lead to an outburst by that individual in terms of aggressive behavior toward some other student in the class, yourself, or specifically toward the individual to whom he initially directed his behavior. It is very easy for a teacher to take off points and to penalize students. It is very difficult to hold back one's temper and not to give in to the desire for revenge. Whatever you do, do not be tempted to penalize a student for your own anger or frustration, although you may think he deserves it.

Chair Throwing

Quite often chair throwing is attention-seeking behavior and should be ignored. When this behavior is directed at an object such as a wall or closet it is almost always attention seeking. However, you must be wary when a child picks up a chair to throw at another child in a fight. In our experience this is usually just a threatening gesture that is rarely carried out. It is certainly a frightening experience but one that should be treated calmly. You can stop such an action by stepping be-between the two children and telling the second child to walk away from the first child to a distant part of the room and reinforce him for that. Without a child to throw it at, the chair will probably be put down or thrown at the floor. This technique takes some sensitivity on the teacher's part to know when the chair will be thrown at a student and when it will not be thrown. In all cases be aware of the possible consequences.

Withdrawal

The shy, withdrawn student is often neglected in the classroom. He is able to blend into the woodwork and escape academic stimulation. If he does not cause any difficulties in the classroom or disturb the teacher, he will most often be viewed as being well adjusted. If he blends well he may even be totally ignored or at least not attended to as often as more vocal students.

What do you do with the withdrawn student? What do you want him to do? What are your terminal objectives for him? Do you want him to talk more, raise his hand, call out, or initiate interactions more frequently with peers? Whatever the objectives are, inform the student of them and place them into an explicitly stated contingency contract with him. By reinforcing such behavior as raising hands, and talking with peers, you are reinforcing behaviors that are incompatible with withdrawal.

For example, tell Debbie that if she raises her hand five times during the day to answer questions, she will receive 5 points or a nickel, or she will be able to take a 5-minute walk, or be otherwise rewarded. When you have observed that the contract can easily be fulfilled, extend the criteria for reinforcement: 20 hand raises, or 10 hand raises plus two self-initiated interactions with a peer will make reinforcement forthcoming. If the criteria are too difficult, backtrack to the point where the child is able to succeed.

It will help Debbie if she has a recording system that she will be able to follow. A simple reinforcement recording system uses a piece of paper placed on the student's desk with two or three headings designating Hand Raising, Self-Initiated Interactions, and a third heading for any other behavior you wish to choose. Each time Debbie emits a certain behavior, she is to mark it on her sheet while you count her behaviors. Your recording system involves a simple check mark or the use of a golf log. This will take you no more than a second, whenever you see Debbie emit the designated behaviors. In this manner you and the student will have an objective measure for reinforcement.

Inadequate Academic Performance

Academic performance can be increased by administering reinforcement contingent on academic output. Instead of reinforcing in-seat attending behavior, inform the students that reinforcement will be contingent on the number of questions or problems answered correctly, or the number of pages read out loud, either alone with the teacher or in a group. It is important that the objective is one that you believe can be attained.

An objective such as "If you read pages five to ten in the *Basal Reader*, silently, then you will receive 10 points," is unrealistic, since you cannot be certain that the objective has been met. The student may indicate that he has read the pages but may have just leafed through them without looking at their content. For this reason you must require a measurable output—"If you read pages five to ten and answer questions one to five in writing, you will receive 10 points." If the questions are based on the reading materials and are answered correctly, you can be fairly sure the material has at least been referred to by the student, although you cannot be certain it was all read prior to answering the questions. Even so, this objective does provide a better indicator of what the student is doing in class, and you will be able to increase the amount and comprehension of such work by making reinforcement contingent on it.

A previous discussion pointed up the inclusion of this technique within a general token economy. It is important to reiterate the necessity of the student working with material at his own level. This aspect of your program should always be checked and rechecked.

Time Out

Time out is a technique that we discussed more fully in Chapter 1. You may find it important to review that technique at this time, as well as the eight guidelines summarized at the end of that chapter.

WORKING WITH OTHER TEACHERS

Often children will learn appropriate behavior in your classroom, but they may have a very hard time carrying this through in other classrooms, such as art or gym or music or science. Quite often the child's inappropriate behavior is a direct function of the kind of contingencies used by the teacher, rather than a result of something inherent in the child. Teachers can be prejudiced or "pick" on children.

Modifying Teacher Behavior

It is possible, however, to give children the ability to modify teacher behavior. We know that your students' appropriate behaviors will extinguish when they leave your class and enter another classroom where the teacher reinforces inappropriate behavior and acts in ways incompatible with those outlined above. A basic survival kit has been prepared to enhance the junior and senior high school students' chances to succeed in future classes (Graubard, Rosenberg, and Miller, 1971). This kit teaches students to modify their teachers' behaviors. With these skills—skills that can change *inappropriate teacher behavior* into appropriate behavior—a student will be able to overcome teacher ineffectiveness and thereby eliminate a critical negative element in his environment.

The following is a synopsis of the method recently employed by seven children, ages twelve to fifteen, in a California junior high school. Each student was responsible for accelerating praise and decelerating negative comments and punishments by their teachers.

1. The children were initially instructed on a one-to-one basis concerning the principles and techniques of behavior modification, as presented in the previous chapter.
2. The children then began to work together and practice these skills through role playing. One student acted as the teacher and the remaining students acted as the class. Techniques that were taught included making eye-contact with teachers and asking for extra help. Children were also taught to make reinforcing comments such as: "Gee, it makes me feel good and I work so much better when you praise me," and "I like the way you teach that lesson." They were taught to sit up straight and nod agreement, contingent on teacher behavior. Students were taught to break eye-contact during scolding and to ignore teachers' provocations, to ask for extra assignments, and to show up early for class.

The teachers in the class were unaware of the program, but the results of the program indicated significant modifications of teachers' behaviors. Other teacher behaviors also changed; they became less punitive and more complimentary to the students.

Teaching students these skills gives them the ability to break down the intransigence and rigidity of some teachers who have not been able to modify their own behavior or take intimations and advice from their colleagues. You can administer a program such as this during the school day. You can teach your students the principles and the techniques just mentioned, and other behaviors that you consider necessary for their survival in future classes. Once the students possess these skills they will be able to modify the behavior of their peers and supervisors, as well as their own behaviors. In addition, you can make entrance into this class and into these lessons contingent on lower probability behavior and lower preference events that usually occur during the day. It is anticipated that lessons presented in this survival kit will be an extremely high preference event for most students.

REVIEW QUESTIONS

1. What are three essential ingredients of a contingency contract?
2. What are some ways that a teacher can get children to return to their work after having received a reinforcement period?
3. One teacher said that she had set up a contingency contract and always used reading as the low preference event and gym as the high preference event in her classroom. Is this a sound strategy?
4. In another classroom the teacher announced to the children that access to recess was contingent on the children's being good. What can the teacher do to improve her classroom practices?
5. A new teacher wanted to learn how to have her children finish all of their academic work during the day and then give them time to play. What would you advise her to do?

6. Johnny had trouble learning multiplication facts. His teacher told his mother that he "had a mental block," and that if he received psychotherapy it would help him in his arithmetic. Would you concur with this recommendation?

7. Gregory and the teacher worked out a contingency contract whereby Gregory would visit the teacher's house after school if he had correctly completed eight pages of arithmetic examples. Gregory did not fulfill his part of the contract. What should the teacher do now?

8. What are some of the advantages of bringing parents into a behavior modification system?

Chapter 4

Observation
and Evaluation

Observational techniques are most often used to ascertain precisely where the student is functioning academically and socially; to find out what effects his environment has on him; and to evaluate any subsequent changes. Observational techniques in the classroom also indicate deficiencies and strengths of teacher performance and point to those areas that require improvement. Numerous observational schedules can be implemented in the classroom and be managed by you and/or your aide or a student. Several of these will be very useful and others may be of little assistance in monitoring your specific requirements. Some of these schedules, particularly those that have been used in research studies, are quite complicated and may require a third party observer. Most teachers do not have the time or opportunity to separate themselves from their class for 10 minutes at a time to collect objective data about their students. To this end several basic observational systems that require little of your time and effort will be discussed.

One goal of observing behavior is to collect unbiased information. Such information is collected when the student is unaware of the fact that he is being observed. For you to observe properly, you must present an image to your students of an individual who is not just watching them. Do not sit in the class with a pencil and paper or a timer and counter as an outside observer would. Continue with your daily activities without appearing to be separate from the classroom.

TOOLS FOR COUNTING THE FREQUENCY OF A BEHAVIOR

There are several instruments that you can use in your observations. The simplest method of observing is counting the frequency of a behavior. Each time a behavior occurs the frequency increases by one. The tools for this type of technique are equally as simple:

Pencil and Paper

Carry a piece of paper on a clipboard or in a book or pad. Have the student's name on it as well as the behavior you have selected to observe for him. Each time the individual emits the behavior, make a mark signifying its occurrence. The number of such marks at the end of each day or at the end of the time interval you have specified indicates the frequency of that behavior.

Golf Log

Use the golf log previously discussed on page 44. While you are engaged in your regular activities you may notice the target behavior, and simply record it.

Since students are curious, and may note what you are doing, it is best to inform them that you will be observing everyone from time to time and will be making a record of your observations. This statement may have a profound effect for a short period, as the children will probably be on their best behavior. But this will soon wear off, and your observational activities will play a very small role in controlling their behaviors.

Electric Counters

Such counters, placed on each student's desk or in an observable place in the room, function similarly to manual counting methods, except that each student is able to monitor his own rates at all times. This method is highly impractical for public schools because of the financial, social, and academic situations that usually prevail.

Counting the frequency of occurrence of *specific behaviors* is the simplest method of observation. Using a golf log, pencil and paper, or an automated frequency counter will provide the same information—the number of times a behavior occurs in a *specified time* or during a specific academic period.

Counting can indicate vital information for students' programs, as the following case study shows.

Case 6
During the 20-minute math lesson Rosa, an extremely withdrawn fourth grader, does not volunteer any answers and does not speak at all, but during the 20-minute reading lesson Rosa talks to people seven times. This pattern is noted to occur, with some variations, *over a period of four consecutive days.* The strategies and program designed for Rosa were based, not upon one observation, but upon four days of watching her. It is very important that program decisions or alterations not be made on the basis of only one observation. Be sure that the behavior occurs at a fairly stable frequency over a longer period of time. The observations of Rosa indicated that her behavior modification program was not necessary for the entire day, but only for the arithmetic lesson, during which she was most withdrawn. We could guess, but we could never really be sure, why she was silent during this period. What is important is that during this period she needed help.

Three important features of all observational systems are indicated in Case 6.

1. The observer *specified* the behavior he was observing. He was observing Rosa's speaking behavior. Speaking was defined beforehand as any verbal statement directed at the teacher or another student.
2. The observer *specified the amount of time* of the observations. The observations were 20 minutes in duration during the math lesson, and 20 minutes during reading.
3. The observer did not rely on only one observation on which to base a program for change. He observed Rosa for *four* 20-minute periods. Relying on only one, two, or three observations to make a decision on program change is not a reliable technique and may lead to false assumptions.

That four observation periods were used in this case does not mean that "four" is a magical number. The number of days chosen as a criterion is dependent on the stability of the behaviors you observe. You cannot determine the number of days you will observe each behavior before your observations actually begin. The number of initial observations on which you will make your decision is determined by the behavioral patterns themselves. This procedure is explained in more detail later in this chapter.

SELECTING AND DEFINING THE TARGET BEHAVIOR

The most important aspects of an observational system are selecting and defining the target behavior. The target behavior should be defined in such a way that anyone observing the student could reliably indicate that the behavior was emitted. If you have selected "Out of Seat" as the target behavior, then this behavior must be precisely delineated for the observer. The observer must know what you mean by "Out of Seat." Is standing next to the chair "Out of Seat?" Is standing next to the desk while reading silently considered "Out of Seat?" What precisely does "Out of Seat" behavior refer to? You must delineate this prior to your observations. Be specific in your definitions.

Now, what is it that you should observe? Each student has a very large repertoire of potential behaviors in the classroom. It is easiest to select initially those behaviors that are "inappropriate" for that time and situation. Yelling during gym time may be appropriate, but during silent reading it is not. Running out of the room, cursing, calling out, fighting, and throwing chairs are a few examples of behaviors that are probably inappropriate. These can be easily selected and defined for observation. You can initially select those behaviors that are most difficult for you to cope with and observe them. (See the checklist on page 99.) (Becker, Madsen, Arnold, and Thomas, 1967.)

Choose a behavior that occurs frequently rather than a behavior that might bother you but occurs only once or twice a week. The latter type of behavior can also be observed and worked with, but it would be better to do so only after you have become proficient with a behavior that occurs more frequently.

Many programs begin by having the teacher choose one or two children in a class. The teacher *specifies one behavior*, such as fighting, leaving the room without permission, cursing, and similar behaviors, and counts it for several days. The teacher also specifies the amount of time for the observations. After the behavior has stabilized and does not vary greatly (see page 109 of this chapter for a discussion of when to initiate the behavior modification program), an academic material analysis (see Chapter 5) to decide whether the material is too difficult or too simple for the student is begun. At this point academic material changes are made and the behavior modification program is specified. During the program the teacher continues to count the frequency of the target behaviors. If they change to a satisfactory level over a period of five to ten days the teacher can be fairly certain she has some control over the problem. If, on the other hand, the behaviors do not decrease or if they increase, then it is time to reevaluate. Look at the curricula materials again for further alteration and also examine the reinforcers in effect. The teacher continues to make changes until control over the problem is achieved. Do not be discouraged by initial failure. Consistent administration of the program and careful analysis of the material should lead to success in terms of decreased inappropriate behaviors and increased appropriate classroom behaviors. You will know if this has occurred by the counts you have taken.

A more precise and useful format in which to integrate the counting procedures is presented below. In this example we selected "running around the room" as a behavior to observe. The fact that Kenny is running around the room is only one aspect of our observations. We also want to know *when* Kenny runs around. Does this behavior occur only during reading or math or art? Does it happen in the mornings, at lunchtime, in the afternoons, or at lineups? Or does he run around all the time regardless of the hour or subject? The answers to these questions will help us to find a pragmatic solution to the problem.

If a child's inappropriate behavior occurs only during an academic subject period he may be communicating that the work is too difficult or too easy for him. When he transmits these signals we check the material he is working on. Perhaps he is correct and the material is too difficult or too easy. The point is to differentiate what effect the child's materials are having on him. Are they punishing him or are they reinforcing him for work? If the materials are too difficult or too easy he is in effect being punished. Punishment is an effective method for producing behavior changes for a short run.

THE BEHAVIORAL ANALYSIS CHART

To give you a better perspective of Kenny's behavior and to present a standardized format for your future observations, we have constructed his Behavioral Analysis Chart (see Figure 7). This chart is based on a simple counting procedure and observations of the consequences of each behavior. It involves a very short period of time and can provide very helpful information. A chart such as this can be constructed for any child in your class for any behavior you want to observe.

BEHAVIORAL ANALYSIS CHART 1

STUDENT'S NAME Kenneth

TEACHER Scott

TARGET BEHAVIOR: Running around room

Date	Subject or Activity	Situation Material	Activity Participants	Consequences	Problems Attempted and Completed Correctly—or Percentage Correct—or Number Pages Read
	Reading Silent = 1 Oral = 2 Math = 3 Social Studies = 4 Art = 5 Lineup = 6	SRA = 1 BASAL = 2 Reading questions = 3 Other = 4	Small groups = 1 Whole class = 2 Individual = 3	Teacher attention = 1 Class attention = 2 Other, specify = 3	
10–11–73	2	2	2	1, 2	
	2	2	2	1, 2	
	2	2	2	2	
	4	4	2	1	
	1	3	3	1	
	1	3	3	3—sat down	0
	3	4	1	1	0

FIGURE 7

Examination of Kenny's Behavioral Analysis Chart (see Figure 7) shows that the chart is divided into four situation variables and also contains a column for indicating what happens to Kenneth after he emits a targeted behavior, as well as his academic achievement for the period. Although there are only six subjects or activities listed on the chart, other subjects germane to your class may be included. Each of the subjects and situations has been coded for quick notation.

The participant variable refers to the type of activity in which the children are required to participate. This category may present useful information about a child's socialization and interaction behaviors. The materials variable refers directly to the name of the material a child is using. You may learn that certain behaviors occur only with one type of material and not with another. Most of these variables can be filled in before the beginning of the lesson. The consequence variable will be determined by what you observe the consequences of behavior to be. Those that are listed here are probably the most frequent and the most general consequences you will observe in the classroom. For example, teacher attention could denote talking, touching, yelling, or physical contact. If there are no apparent teacher or class consequences to the child's action, then take note of what the child does after the behavior is completed. Does he sit down, curse, or use another inappropriate behavior?

Use of this chart allows you to be aware of your own responses to the child and gives you an indication of how to deal with specific problems. Each time Kenneth "runs around the room" it is indicated by using the code under the *Subject or Activity* variable. On 10–11–73 Kenneth ran around the room seven times. Each entry under *Subject or Activity* indicates that the targeted behavior has occurred once. In Kenneth's case he ran around the room three times during oral reading, once during social studies, twice during silent reading, and once during math.

There is additional space on the chart to indicate, in summary form, the student's academic performance during each period.

Kenneth's behavioral analysis chart tells us a great deal about his behavioral repertoire. On 10–11–73 the teacher in this example noticed Kenny running around the room seven times. Each time such behavior was observed the teacher filled in the next appropriate row on the chart. The clerical work for each observation took no longer than 5 seconds. On this day Kenny's inappropriate behavior was not specific to any one subject, time, or activity. At first it appeared that nothing was consistent about his behavior. However, examining the consequences of his behavior reveals that on six of the seven occasions that Kenny behaved inappropriately either the teacher or his classmates reinforced his behavior. In other words, Kenny was reinforced 86 percent of the time that he was disruptive. It is very probable that he would persist in running as long as these consequences continued. After several days of observation it became necessary to institute a behavior modification program for Kenny.

Let us look at another example. A teacher reported that Cynthia sits in her seat in the back of the room and *hardly ever* says anything or raises her hand to answer a question. "Hardly ever" is an inadequate description of her behavior, and we must have more precise information. The behaviors to observe are hand raising and number of social interactions. Observation showed that Cynthia did not raise her hand at all during reading, social studies, or art, but she did raise her hand during the math period. The first inference that might be drawn is that Cynthia liked math and was therefore responsive. That may be true, but saying that someone *likes* math does not help in analyzing the behavior. Why does Cynthia raise her hand? Observation (see Figure 8) reveals that Cynthia is called on 60 percent of the time when she raises her hand. She receives attention plus any praise the teacher might extend for answering the question. In addition Cynthia probably knows the answer, which is reinforcing in itself. It is reasonable to assume that if the teacher stops calling on her when her hand is raised the behavior would extinguish and she might try another way to get the teacher's attention or else she might withdraw. This information would be found in Cynthia's behavior analysis

BEHAVIORAL ANALYSIS CHART 2

STUDENT'S NAME Cynthia   TARGET BEHAVIOR: Raising hand

TEACHER Simon

Date	Subject or Activity	Situation Material	Activity Participants	Consequences	Problems Attempted and Completed Correctly—or Percentage Correct
	Reading Silent = 1 Oral = 2 Math = 3 Social Studies = 4 Art = 5 Lineup = 6	SRA = 1 BASAL = 2 Other = 3	Small groups = 1 Whole class = 2 Individual = 3	Teacher attention = 1 Class attention = 2 Other, specify = 3	
12–14–73	3 3 3		2 2 1	1, 2 1, 2 1, 2	attempted: 16 correct: 15
12–15–73	3 3 3		2 2 1	1, 2 3—lowers hand 3—lowers hand	attempted: 34 correct: 29

FIGURE 8

chart. An additional piece of information to note is that Cynthia is completing a high number of arithmetic problems with a high accuracy score.

Upon further observation you will notice that Cynthia does not receive attention nor does she raise her hand during reading or social studies. What are the consequences of sitting quietly and not raising one's hand? Some hypothetical consequencies might be staring out of the window, not being noticed and escaping, or reading a comic book, or other actions. A useful procedure for dealing with this type of classroom problem is to (1) examine the academic materials that the child is using (refer to the chart on academic materials in Chapter 5), (2) make an hypothesis concerning the consequences of the behavior (e.g., is teacher nonattention maintaining this behavior?), (3) test your hypothesis by designing a program. Would a contingency contract for hand raising be sufficient? Perhaps, but you will not know until you have tried.

A number of exercises have been provided in this chapter for you to complete.

Exercise 1 This exercise is designed to give you practice in the use of the Behavioral Analysis Chart

Figure 9 shows a Behavioral Analysis Chart that you can use in your class. Select one child in your class whose behavior problem is being out of his seat frequently, talking at inappropriate times and without permission, or any other behavior. Observe the student for several days using the Behavioral Analysis Chart. At the end of this time make an initial hypothesis as to what is maintaining the behavior. The Behavioral Analysis Chart should be used for one student at a time. Whenever you notice the child engaging in the specific behavior, record the data called for in the specified column. An aide may assist you and perhaps spend a designated time each day recording the students' behavior with these charts as guides. A student from your class or from a higher grade can also do the job.

BEHAVIORAL ANALYSIS CHART 3

STUDENT'S NAME _____   TARGET BEHAVIOR: _____

TEACHER _____

Date	Subject or Activity	Situation Material	Activity Participants	Consequences	Problems Attempted and Completed Correctly—or Percentage Correct
	Reading Silent = 1 Oral = 2 Math = 3 Social Studies = 4 Art = 5 Lineup = 6	SRA = 1 BASAL = 2 Other = 3	Small groups = 1 Whole class = 2 Individual = 3	Teacher attention = 1 Class attention = 2 Other, specify = 3	

FIGURE 9

THE BECKER BEHAVIORAL CHECKLIST

The Becker Behavioral Checklist (see Figure 10) is an excellent example of a teacher's categorizing behaviors so as to make observation that much clearer. In selecting categories of behaviors to observe and record Becker et al. (1967) followed several general rules:

1. The categories should reflect behaviors which interfered with classroom learning and/or,
2. They should involve behaviors which violated the rules for permissible behavior established by the teacher and/or students.
3. They should reflect particular behaviors a teacher and/or a child wanted to change [e.g., thumbsucking]. . . .
4. The classes of behavior should be mutually exclusive.
5. The definition must refer to observables and not involve inferences.
6. The number of [categories] should not exceed ten [pp. 289–290].

No. of 20-second intervals / Names of pupils	1st	2d	3d	4th	5th	6th	etc.
REIS, R	SNT	XA	BS	X-AB	X-AB X	SNT	
JONES, C	B	B	BN	B	S	S	
SMITH, J	TA	TA	T	A	TS	TA	
etc.							

FIGURE 10 *The Becker Behavioral Checklist.* A sample observation matrix showing codification of child's behavior over time. Adapted from Becker, Madsen, Arnold, and Thomas (1967). Key: A—disturbing others directly and aggression; B—blurting out, commenting, and vocal noise; AF—fighting; L—looking; N—disruptive noise made by striking objects; S—relevant behavior; T—talking; X—gross motor behaviors; X-AB—walked out of room.

Categorizing and coding behaviors in a manner similar to the Becker Behavioral Checklist makes observational systems less cumbersome and more adaptable to each teacher's specific requirements.

RATE OF PROBLEMS SOLVED

One method of analyzing academic behavior is to calculate the rate of problems solved correctly. To do this, instruct the child to write the time he started working on his paper, and the time he stopped working. If your children cannot tell time use a digital clock from which they merely have to copy the numbers that appear on the clock face. Once the time started and time stopped have been written down it is a simple matter to compute the elapsed time. Thus, if the child starts to do SRA problems at 10:20 and stops at 10:57 you would subtract the difference between 57 and 20 and ascertain that the child worked on the problems for 37 minutes. The next step is to add the number of problems solved correctly, and then divide the total time spent on doing the problems into the number of problems solved correctly. If the child completes 74 problems in 37 minutes this would work out to the rate of two problems a minute. Such a procedure is called a *rate measure*, and it is a good indicator of pupil progress. (See page 120 for another use of rate.)

Not all curriculum areas lend themselves as readily to computing rate measures as does SRA. However, it is possible to train students to keep these and similar data, and to set up their own charts and graphs. Graphing their own behaviors can be used as a reinforcer for your students. Learning how to use graphs can be employed as a high preference event in your class.

Data such as these may be easily incorporated into the Behavioral Analysis Chart.

Although rate is a very frequently used measure of academic behavior, it does have several disadvantages.

In the example, above, the student was answering two questions per minute. If he had worked for 90 minutes, it is possible that his rate would remain at two per minute. He is thus answering more problems and taking more time, but his rate remains the same. It is possible that the rate of correct answers would also remain the same. There is a piece of helpful information that is easily obtainable but is missing from this analysis. That information is the percent of problems correct.

PERCENT OF PROBLEMS SOLVED CORRECTLY

By including the "percent of problems solved correctly" as an additional measure the analysis of the student's problem is more complete. The use of percentage correct substitutes quality of response for speed response. That is, the behavior to be reinforced is no longer dependent on speed but rather on accuracy. In effect, the teacher would be saying, "I would rather the student get more problems correct than just do more problems faster, irrespective of accuracy." We are no longer solely interested in the rate of correctly completing math problems but instead in the accuracy of completion.

The problem that arises with the use of this measure is that some students may answer very few questions and get them all correct, but in doing so use all the time allotted to them. That is, a student may take 45 minutes to answer only four mathematics problems because he is being reinforced for accuracy, not quantity of responses. What is needed is a method that combines both speed and accuracy.

The answer to the problem lies in a combination of the two measures. If both a rate measure and a percentage measure for academic behavior and social behavior are taken, then an adequate amount of information upon which to make any necessary program changes will be available. It then becomes a simple matter of consequating both types of behaviors. Reinforcers can be programmed so as to be contingent on both increased rate and increased or high accuracy levels. By integrating the two measures, any pitfalls in the use of a single indicator can be avoided.

TIME SAMPLING—OBSERVING
LARGE GROUPS OF STUDENTS

It is a relatively simple matter to count and record the behavior of one or two students in a class at any given time. However, there is a problem when observations are needed of a large group of students in a class in which the teacher has a limited amount of assistance.

Observing During Brief Periods Daily

In situations such as these it is equally impossible to observe only one student all day or every student in class for a full day. Several procedures based on sampling techniques can be used. The technique used to overcome this problem is to select, or sample, brief periods during the day that are representative of those periods you are interested in, and observe the students during this time. By selecting a limited number of periods it is possible to get a very good overview of what the student is doing in class.

Taking a Reading

One quick and efficient technique to be used in large classes is to "Take a Reading" on the class. At selected intervals count the number of students in the class who are following directions and are emitting appropriate behavior. By selecting several intervals during the day, which are actually samples of all possible intervals, and counting the number of students who are behaving appropriately, the teacher can get a good picture of the general behavior level of the class. In addition, by taking readings on the class at several intervals during the program the teacher is able to follow any general changes in levels of behavior as a function of changes in the programs used.

The simplest way to evaluate the behavior counts is to transform them into percentages. The percentage figures refer to the proportion of students in the class who are following directions and are meeting the momentary objectives the teacher has set.

Exercise 2 This exercise is to give you practice in Taking a Reading.

Prior to class select several intervals during the day for taking a reading. At that time look around the room, observe and count the number of students who are emitting appropriate behavior. Write down the count you get and save it for future use and comparison. Take several readings until you feel comfortable in using this method.

A more precise, although more complex, method of sampling behavior is to observe each student in the class individually or in small groups for specified periods of time. By using the techniques outlined below it is possible not only to take readings on small groups of students but also to focus on the observation of specific types of behaviors or group interactions. One such method is "counting split classes." The advantage of this method is that you can end up observing each child in your class and, because of the systematic way in which you are observing, you will not miss any one child. Another advantage of this method is that you can use the observation of several of the clusters as a sampling of your entire class.

Counting Split Classes

Another technique for sampling behaviors in a large class, which is more complex than Taking a Reading, is using split classes.

1. Split your class into equal sets of three to four students each (just for observation purposes). With a class of thirty you may have as many as ten groups. This is similar to our division of the class into two groups for the "good behavior" game (p. 73). To facilitate matters, group children who sit together or near each other into sets. This will reduce the time needed to search for each child when he is to be observed. Rather than observing the entire class, you now have to observe only three or four children during each observation period.

2. Begin by specifying one behavior for each student you will observe. Be sure you have precisely defined the behavior you intend to observe. For example, if you select out-of-seat behaviors for John, then you must know which specific behaviors denote being out of his seat. Does standing near his desk and having one foot on his chair constitute being out of his seat, or not?

3. Use either the simple counting procedures (Taking a Reading) or, if possible, the Behavioral Analysis Chart. It may be advisable to use the counting procedure and fill in the chart after the observation period is completed.

For teachers who interact with students for an entire day:

4. Select a number of 5- or 10-minute intervals during the day that equal the number of sets you have grouped. With eight sets you should select eight 5- to 10-minute segments during the day. Since it is very difficult for teachers to keep track of all temporal intervals during the day, these segments should be keyed by a very definite environmental stimulus in the school, such as the school bell at the start of each period. The bell is a signal for you. It tells you that you are to observe one of the sets for the next 5 or 10 minutes. The order for observing each set is left to you. It can be random or according to a specific plan. In this manner, after five days you will have had 25 to 50 minutes of observation for each child in your class. These five days should give you a good representation of each student's classroom behavior. Again, five days is not a magical number. Continue your observations until you note stable and regular patterns so as to make precise decisions.

If you are particularly concerned about the behaviors of just a few students, you can observe these particular sets of children a few times during the day without taking data on other groups of children. It is usually necessary to make some kind of compromise in collecting data; if you take data on many students, you will have to restrict the number of times and behaviors that you can observe. If you are interested in just a few students, it is possible to observe much more often and gather information about many kinds of behaviors.

    5. After observing each set, record the academic materials that the student was using, or was supposed to be using, and the count of the behavior.

    6. Continue to observe the student as unobtrusively as possible after the behavior modification program is begun.

Using an Aide or Student to Observe

In many schools a teacher has a class for only one 45-minute period a day. In these cases the observational objectives and techniques are different. If you interact with the students for only one period a day (45 minutes), the task of observing and recording the behavior of a class of 20 to 30 students *by yourself* is very difficult unless you use time-sampling techniques like Taking a Reading. The problem is greatly alleviated if you have an aide to help you, or if you could train one of your students to take data on the remainder of the class. (You should be aware that such a student activity can be a very powerful reinforcer.) If this is possible several alternative observational schedules are available to you.

    If the aide's time during class is taken up by observing, it will still be worthwhile for you and your students. Such observation will make you more aware of the students' reactions to you, to each other, and to the material. This method enables you to continually reevaluate the students' behaviors and to be prepared to alter behavioral contingencies for them in order to help them learn social and academic skills.

    Objections to Observation by an Aide When the observation situation is posed to a teacher, two objections are usually raised: (1) "I don't like being observed and evaluated by anyone else; I don't even like it when my supervisor observes me; and (2) "My aide has other things to do and her supervisor won't understand if she is not helping the children during the period."

Regarding the first objection, it should be understood that *it is not the teacher that is being evaluated, but the methods employed.* In this case it is the children's behavior that is being observed and that is to be altered. The observations indicate what must be changed or continued in the environment. No evaluative or judgmental statements are made concerning teacher ability, style, or personality. No one but the teacher and aide need ever review the data collected. The observations yield objective information and offer suggestions for running the class, nothing more and nothing less.

The second objection is more serious, and concerns the relative importance of observation as contrasted with the time an aide could spend teaching children in a one-to-one interaction. An aide's observation of student behavior does not eliminate the possibility of working with individuals when the observations are completed. Specific observation is crucial to the success of your program. Although an aide may not be in direct contact with the child during this time, she is in a sense helping to plan his future curriculum and behavioral contingencies, and the importance of such activities should not be discounted.

Your aide or a student can use any of the third party observational systems explained below.

THIRD PARTY OBSERVATION SYSTEMS

1. *Counting.* Behaviors of children are counted by a third party in a similar manner to that indicated above.
2. Use of the *Behavioral Analysis Chart* as indicated above.
3. *The Becker Behavioral Checklist* (Figures 10 and 11 are two ways of depicting this checklist).

   The observational system for the Becker Checklist is divided into 20-second intervals. The behaviors the observer is to observe are coded on the left margin. You can add any idiosyncratic behaviors of students to be observed to the list. Similarly, you may alter the time intervals to 10 seconds, 30 seconds, or longer.

THE BECKER BEHAVIORAL DATA COLLECTION MATRIX

NAME _____   DATE _____

OBSERVER _____   TIME—begin _____

                                         end _____

Time interval ⟶	20 sec.	20 sec.	20 sec.	⟶			⟶
A							
AF							
B							
L							
N							
O							
S							
T							
X							
X-AB							

Key: A—disturbing others directly and aggression; B—blurting out, commenting. and vocal noise; AF—fighting; L—looking; N—disruptive noise made by striking objects; O—other; S—relevant behavior; T—talking; X—gross motor behaviors; X-AB—walked out of room.

FIGURE 11

The observer is seated in the rear of the room with stopwatch, checklist, and pencil. Once the watch is started the observer is to view one student for 20 seconds and then record these behaviors during the next 10 seconds. At the start of the next 20-second interval, the observer again observes the same child for 20 seconds and records for the following 10 seconds.

An alternative procedure to observing the same student for the entire specified time interval (e.g., three minutes) is to observe each child in consecutive order. After one 20-second observation for each child, the observer begins again with the first child in the class until each child has been observed for the specified time period. Each alternative will provide similar data, although the first method presents a smoother and more even flow of individual behavior. The result of such observations will be frequency counts of the specific behaviors that you are interested in, and also percentages of appropriate and inappropriate behavior.

Case 7

Ron's behavior was observed for 3 minutes (nine 20-second intervals), and recorded on the Becker Checklist. During these nine observation intervals it was observed that Ron attended to task three times, was out of his seat three times, and was staring into space three times. The data tell us that Ron is attending to his material only one-third of the time he is in class. The data also inform us that a specified contingency for being in his seat is needed to reduce the out-of-seat problem. Once he is at least in his seat we can begin to set contingencies for academic behavior while in his seat. Beginning with the student at the level of his current functioning, we will first manage his sitting behavior, then his attending, and finally his rate and percent of work output. We can ascertain our degree of success by examining the data regarding Ron's behavior.

Exercise 3   This exercise is designed to give your aide or observer practice in using the Becker Behavioral Checklist.

Your aide should be seated in the rear of the room out of direct contact with the students in your class. The aide should have several copies of the checklist, a pencil, and a watch with a second hand or a stopwatch. At the outset of the interval the stopwatch is started, and the aide observes the first student for 20 seconds. After 20 seconds your aide has 10 seconds to record what he/she has observed. After a greater amount of practice, if desired, the aide can shorten the observation interval to 10–15 seconds. Depending on which alternative observation interval has been selected, your aide is to proceed in this manner until the observation interval has been completed. At this time record the data that has been collected.

WHEN TO INTRODUCE THE BEHAVIOR MODIFICATION SYSTEM

In some of the examples given to this point, the authors have made reference to initiating behavior modification programs after specified periods of time (e.g., three days or four days). It was pointed out that these are not "magic numbers" for initiating an intervention program, and that the final decision should be based on the behavioral patterns of the children in your class. The rationale for waiting until there are specific types of behavioral patterns is to be sure that the program that is introduced is the "real" cause of any change in behavior. It is imperative to be certain that the behavior is under control of the behavior modification methods and not a function of chance or external factors. This is important because you may want to repeat your procedures on a different class of behaviors for the same child or a different child. You will want to know that your procedure was effective and that the change did not occur fortuitously.

Prior to introducing an intervention program the behaviors that are being observed should reflect stable and systematic movement. Figure 12 demonstrates a fairly stable baseline. (Baseline refers to the period of time during which no behavior modification program is in effect. Any later changes in behavior will be contrasted with the baseline period.)

During the first seven days of baseline the student was out of his seat an average of 4.3 times per period. There is very little variability in behavior during the first seven days, and it is assumed that this level would remain stable if no intervention had begun. An intervention program was begun on the eighth day. Any subsequent changes in behavior could, with several reservations, be reliably attributed to the program in effect.

If there is a specific trend in the data, then the intervention should be introduced only if an opposite effect is

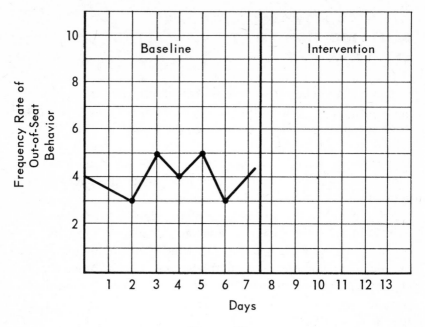

FIGURE 12

expected. Figure 13 illustrates two opposing trends during baseline. Trend "A" is an *accelerating* behavioral rate, and an intervention program would be introduced only if the objective is to suppress the behavior. Trend "B" is a *decelerating* behavioral rate, and an intervention program would be introduced only if the objective is to strengthen the behavior.

If Trend "A" is an accelerating Out of Seat rate then an intervention program to suppress this rate would be introduced. However, if the behavior in question was "Number of math problems answered correctly," then an intervention program might not be introduced, since increased rates could be expected even without it. In the same regard a decelerating "Fighting" rate (Trend "B") may indicate there is no need for an intervention program, while a decelerating academic rate does indicate a need.

Of course, not all situations are as clear-cut as those shown in Figures 12 and 13. There may be cases in which there is no trend indicated, or a case in which a stable baseline

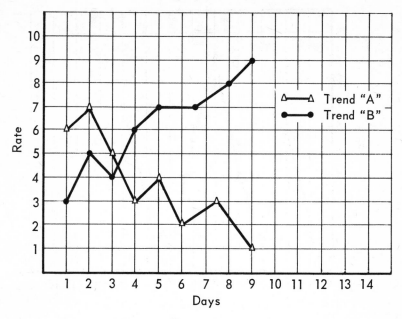

FIGURE 13

rate is not indicated. Such a situation is demonstrated in Figure 14. It is evident from the figure that the student's behavior rate is erratic and not under the control of any environmental stimuli. If an intervention program were initiated at this point, it is possible that the behavior rate would stabilize. The stabilization and subsequent behavioral control would thus be a function of the intervening behavior modification program. Had the program not been initiated it is difficult to determine if the behavior would have stabilized anyway. Nevertheless, if you are confronted with a situation such as that in Figure 14 and you can no longer delay instituting a behavior modification program, then do so; but, be aware of possibly false conclusions.

NONDIRECTIVE OBSERVATIONS

There are other types of data collection systems that do not require daily supervision and attention and that can provide an indication of the socialization experience each student is

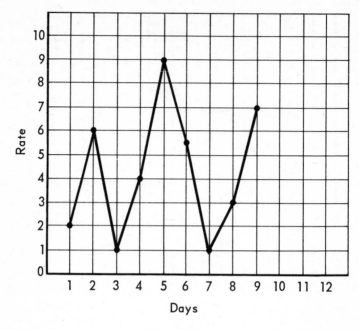

Figure 14

undergoing. We will discuss some of these instruments; however, we recommend that their use should only be supplementary to the direct observation system.

Sociograms

The sociogram is a method by which you can identify social groupings, leadership hierarchies, and personal preferences and antagonisms. A simple technique is to ask your students to select those peers within the class with whom they would like to sit, play, and work. Inform them that the groups they are being asked to arrange will be used for a specific assignment in class. Each student may select from one to four peers for his group. Be cautious of arousing undue anxiety among the students because of the ratings, and be sure to indicate that all ratings will be kept secret.

Once you have collected these ratings you can either plot them into sociograms or present them descriptively. Both methods provide the same information, although the former is more dramatic. (See Figure 15.) When you plot the data, arrows are drawn from one person to another indicating preference. A double arrow indicates mutual preference—that is, a double arrow between John and Eddie would indicate that they both prefer each other. Rejections and antagonisms are indicated by the absence of such arrows toward the student.

This technique can be incorporated into a behavior management system as a secondary source of information. For example, if Dean and Al have a mutual preference to sit together, such an arrangement could be made contingent on completing a target behavior; for example, "If you both finish

Diagramatic Sketch of Sociogram Data

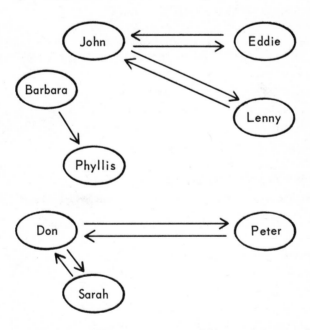

FIGURE 15   *Explanation of Sociogram.* John, Eddie, and Lenny all express mutual preferences for one another. Barbara expresses preference for Phyllis but it is not mutual. Lenny and Phyllis do not prefer each other, nor do Sarah and Peter. Don is preferred by both Sarah and Peter.

the math lesson with a grade of 80 percent correct, then you can sit together for 45 minutes." Such arrangements can be drawn from the sociogram data. In addition, contingencies for withdrawn students can also be arranged from such data. Taking new sociograms several times during the year will afford you a better view of the classroom environment and will allow you to make the necessary alterations in the behavioral modification system in effect. Frequent sociograms will let you track changes in preferences and antagonisms.

Although it is often true that teachers "know" that these relationships occur, this method—a simple and effective method of collecting such information—provides a more objective basis for your conclusions.

Academic Achievement Tests

A number of standardized achievement tests in reading, math, and other subjects are available to you. The best evaluation of them can be found in the *Mental Measurements Yearbook* (Buros, 1972). If you use these achievement tests, they should be considered as a gross indicator of an individual's academic level, subject to a great deal of error. They must be followed by your own individual observation and evaluation of the student's behavioral and academic repertoire. In several studies teacher-made achievement tests have been found to be more valid indicators of student ability than standardized tests. It is advisable to make use of them.

OBSERVING THE TEACHER

To this point we have discussed methods for observing students in the classroom. Student-teacher interaction is one of the most crucial aspects of teaching. By making the teacher aware of these interactions and providing a system for self-assessment, the teacher will be able to modify her own behaviors. One such method is Spence's (1972) *Pupil-Teacher Interaction Compliance Pinpoints.*

Spence's Pupil-Teacher Interaction Compliance Pinpoints

Spence's interaction methodology focuses on interactions between the child's behavior and the teacher's reaction to it, which might serve to modify that behavior. The frequencies of occurrence are recorded daily, using standardized charts that allow the teacher to see her own progress. Teachers chart their own progress based on their own observations or on observations made by others (aide, student, or other individual).

Unlike other interaction analyses, Spence's techniques have been adapted precisely for token economy and contingency management procedures and therefore can be helpful to your analysis of your own behaviors within such a system. For example, this system can inform you whether or not you respond to hand-raising, call-out, or out-of-seat behavior, if you praise, administer tokens contingent on appropriate behaviors, and so forth. Follow-up on your part on such information will help you to administer your own system. Figure 16 is an adaptation of Spence's *Pupil-Teacher Interaction Compliance Pinpoints*. After you familiarize yourself with the categories you may wish to test it out or use it in your classroom.

In Spence's interaction matrix the names of specific pupils and the target behaviors that you wish to modify are listed in the left-hand column. Specific teacher responses are indicated in the top column. Examples of teacher responses might include ignoring verbal praise, tokens, verbal reprimand, contingency setting, time out, and others. A tally mark is then placed in the square where the specific teacher response to the target behavior interacts. At the end of a specified observation period the tallies can be converted into a rate measure.

ANALYZING THE DATA

We have consistently referred to the need for basing decisions on data collected during observation periods. The procedures

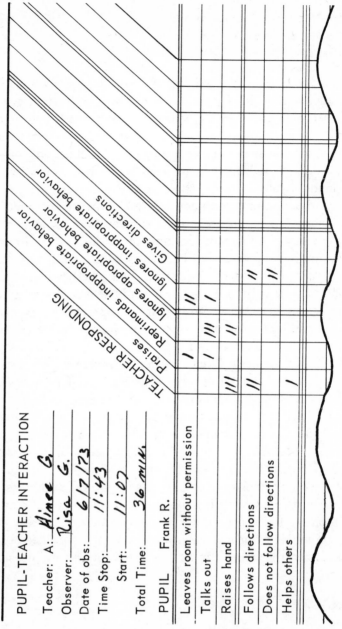

FIGURE 16 Adapted from Spence (1972).

and decisions for introducing behavior modification systems were based on such observations. The decision-making process was simplified by use of an objective method of recording and presenting the data graphically.

A visual representation of the data enhances the decision-making process regarding the program, and enables others to quickly decipher patterns and trends that may be developing. Rather than relying solely on symmetrical and precise columns of numerical data that have been systematically collected but that can still obfuscate the problem, it is recommended that the data be transformed into equally systematically prepared graphs which are easily analyzed.

SUMMARY DATA COLLECTION

After collecting the data, whether from the Becker Checklist, the Behavioral Analysis Chart, Spence's Pinpoints, academic achievement, or simple counting, it is necessary to record them in a summarized form. Rather than having to rely on storing hundreds of individual observation sheets and having the difficult task of locating specific data sheets when you are analyzing the data, it is recommended that summary data sheets be compiled. Although the type of data collected is specific to each program, there are several procedures that should be followed in all programs.

Figure 17 is a typical summary data collection table. After each observation period the observer collates all the material and enters the information in the appropriate columns. Figure 17 is partly based on the Becker Behavioral Checklist and therefore Becker's coding categories for social behaviors are used. These categories can be altered for any specific behaviors being observed. Again, the rationale is to have a summary table containing all the information needed for further analysis without having to refer to each individual observation sheet. Once the data are in summary form they can be used for any type of analyses, including graphing.

STUDENT'S NAME _____

Date	Elapsed Time	Subject/ Activity	Phase	Social Behaviors [frequency]					Academic Behavior				Observer's Name
				Inappropriate	Appropriate				# Attempted	# Correct	% Correct	% Time Attending	
				R	X	T	A	I					

FIGURE 17

Graphing

A graph is a schematic and pictorial representation of an individual's behavior. It allows you to make objective statements and decisions based on the data presented and also depicts the data in a clear, visual manner. There are several types of graphs that can be useful to you: (1) line graphs—often called frequency polygons; (2) bar graphs; and (3) cumulative frequency recordings. Line graphs will probably be most useful to you.

> *Exercise 4—Line graphs*   Draw two axes on a sheet of graph paper similar to those in Figure 18. The abscissa, or horizontal axis, should be labeled with your time interval (days, hours, minutes, and so on). If you observe each student for 10 minutes each day, the abscissa can be labeled "Days," with the number of responses for that 10-minute period representing one day. The ordinate, or vertical axis, is labeled as the rate, percentage, or frequency of the target behavior. For example, the ordinate in Figure 18 represents the number of times the individual was observed to be fighting.
>
> Once the axes are labeled, mark off equal distances on each axis. On the frequency axis, you can make each occurrence of a behavior equal to five boxes, two boxes, or one box on the graph paper. Whichever ratio you decide on, be consistent. Similarly, on the time axis, each date interval must be the same throughout the graph.
>
> *Plotting the data.*   First, refer to your summary data table. On your graph locate the intersection point between the first date and the frequency count for that same date. Make a dot on the graph at that point. Locate the next intersection point between the second date and the frequency count for that same date. Do the same thing for each successive date for which you have a count. A zero count is also recorded should that occur. Once the points have been plotted, join them by a straight line connecting each successive point, as in Figure 18. The completed graph is a line graph, often called the frequency polygon.
>
> Look at Figure 18. Days 1 through 7 represent Teddy's *baseline* of solving arithmetic problems correctly— prior to instituting any behavior modification program. Teddy had four days when he did not solve any problems

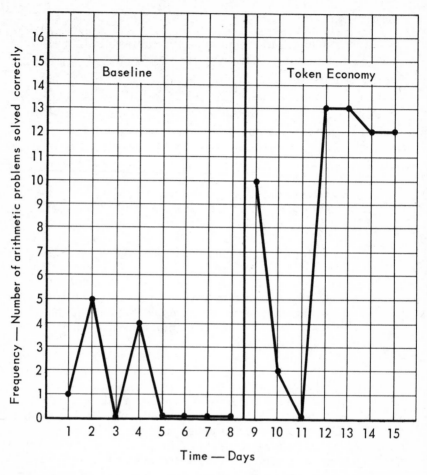

FIGURE 18

correctly (days 4–7), and it is clear from the graph that Teddy's arithmetic behavior is a frequent problem that requires a solution. (Teddy's average rate of solving arithmetic problems is only two problems per day during baseline. See the discussion of rate on page 100.)

On day 8 a token economy was introduced for Teddy. (It is noted by a line separating the two phases. Such a separation should always be used and labeled as in Figure 18.) His average rate of solving arithmetic problems over the next eight days increased to seven per day.

Note that the graph indicates zero rates for four of the first eight days. On days 9 and 11 Teddy's rate decelerated to preprogram levels. This performance can be considered a testing period. When the teacher consistently reinforced appropriate behavior, and did not attend to dawdling, his arithmetic problem-solving rate increased dramatically (days 12–15).

The advantage of presenting the data graphically is the ability to "see" this pattern in a simplified manner and to make decisions on it. This type of graph can be incorporated and used for almost all the behavioral observation systems discussed to this point—counting, Becker's Checklist, the Behavioral Analysis Chart, Spence's Pupil-Teacher Interaction Compliance Pinpoints, and others. Using it often will help you program for students in your class and should be an integral part of any behavior modification program you institute.

It is also possible to depict two or more behaviors on the same graph by coding the specific classes of behavior you wish to denote—for example, fighting might be coded with a square, and hand raises with a circle (see Figure 19). Notice that the use of a broken line and a solid line makes it easier to read, but it is not necessary to use this specific technique.

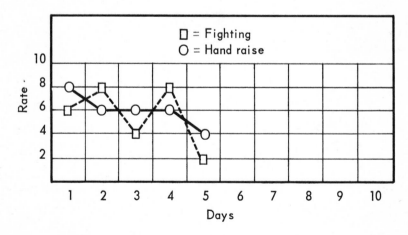

Figure 19

For review questions, we have prepared two short exercises in graphing behaviors. We think your completion of them will reinforce what you have read in this chapter.

REVIEW QUESTIONS

1. The frequency counts of Kathy's calling-out behavior during three weeks in school, and the frequency counts of the teacher's responding to her are indicated in the summary table (Figure 20a). Plot the data for both teacher and Kathy on graph paper (Figure 20b). Use different symbols to distinquish the behaviors. Label both ordinates. Label baseline and intervention phases. Indicate a code for symbols used. The answers are to be found in Appendix B.

2. See Appendix B for the answers to this exercise.
   (1) During the first five days plotted there was no program in effect. This period of time called _____.
   (2) During the first five days there appears to be a relationship between Kathy's behavior and _____.

Date	# Call-Outs	# Times Teacher Responded
1/2/73	12	9
1/3	14	10
1/4	8	6
1/5	17	14
1/6	15	13
1/9	8	3
1/10	10	6
1/11	7	2
1/12	7	3
1/13	4	0
1/16	8	0
1/17	2	1
1/18	4	0
1/19	2	0
1/20	2	0

FIGURE 20a   Question 1—Summary Table

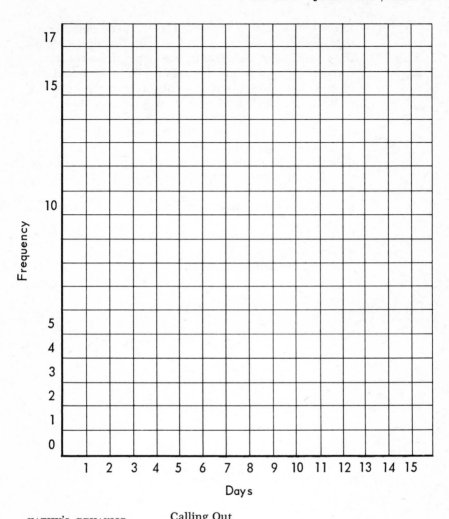

KATHY'S BEHAVIOR ___Calling Out_____

TEACHER'S BEHAVIOR___Responding to Calling Out_____

FIGURE 20b   Graph of Kathy's and Teacher's Behavior

(3) The teacher was observed to attend to a high percentage of Kathy's behavior during the baseline period. She decided she would _____ Kathy's calling out.

(4) On the sixth day we notice that the teacher's behavior decreased. She was trying to _____ Kathy's behavior by ignoring it.

(5) Extinction is a slow process. The teacher's nonattention to Kathy when she called out had the effect of decreasing the frequency of calling out. It was not, however, totally successful. Which of the following steps would you recommend taking to supplement this teacher's program?

a. Reinforce a behavior that was incompatible with calling out—e.g., sitting quietly.
b. Check the level of the curriculum materials.
c. Check on peer reinforcement.
d. Institute contingency contracts.
e. Time out during disruptive periods.
f. Send for mother.
g. Yell at Kathy for being disrespectful after all the effort you've put in.
h. Send for the principal.
i. Give up.
j. Check available reinforcers.

Chapter 5

Curriculum and Behavioral Objectives

Curriculum is an essential component and probably the most crucial ingredient of any behavior modification system in the schoolroom. Too many teachers reinforce passive behavior rather than the actual demonstration of learning; and too often inadequate or insufficient learning can be traced to a teacher's setting objectives in terms that are more concerned with personality characteristics than with learning. This is often the result of stating objectives in terms so general that they can be defined only philosophically.

STATING OBJECTIVES AND CRITERIA

For example, one teacher set as her objective that the children in her class learn two things: first, to be "creative" and, second, "to work up to their potential." The word "creative" is so subjective that virtually anything that is done could come under this rubric, and hence the teacher would not be able to reinforce differentially any specific behavior to shape creativity. The second objective is stated in such a way that it defies analysis and planning. Philosophers, psychologists, and psychometricians have never been able to define "potential" to their own satisfaction. In what area does the teacher mean the word? Certainly we are all potential liars and potential thieves and potential misfits, but it is doubtful that these potentials are something that the teacher has in mind as an objective to "work up to." And who is to decide what the potential is—the teacher or the children? These are only some of the questions brought to mind by such generalized objectives. The two objectives, so stated, are essentially unmeasurable. The teacher will not be in a position to change her strategy, tactics, and curriculum material if children do not reach her stated objectives.

At other times objectives are stated more specifically, with subject matter in mind, but criteria are stated subjectively. Examples of such statements of objectives would be: "to learn reading skills," or "to understand algebra principles," or "to appreciate music," or "to know the causes of the Civil War." Terms such as "to know," "to appreciate," "to understand," and similar ones, describe internal processes that can only be inferred. Who is to say what it is to appreciate something; who is to determine whether or not a child appreciates music, and how will anyone know? What kind of music does the teacher want "appreciated?" Would an "appreciation" of rock music satisfy the stated objective? Sometimes course objectives are similarly written in such forms as "to teach thinking," "to acquire healthy attitudes," "to develop positive mental health," and others like these, but these are equally subjective statements. When objectives are stated with subjective criteria, they do not lend themselves to good teaching, since no one— teacher or pupil—can be sure just what the learner has to do or what skills should result as a function of teaching. In addition, if the criteria are not more clear-cut, a teacher can end up reinforcing exactly the opposite learning behaviors of those she intends to instill.

The best way to avoid this kind of murkiness is to state objectives behaviorally. This means that the learner will have to display a behavior that is the criteria measure of whether he has the ability to use the skill in question. The behavior display will have to be overt, unambiguous, and specific. The pupil is required to engage in an observable act or leave some observable product. Therefore statements of behavioral objectives call for use of such terms as "to identify," "to list," "to describe," "to translate," "to demonstrate"; or for the use of such phrases as "to answer a specific number of questions at a specific rate." Such terms are quite different from those discussed above: "to know," "to appreciate," "to understand," and so on. In order to show how to make the criteria of objectives more explicit, we can break down some general teaching objectives into behavioral objectives. For the purposes of such an exercise we can use both academic and social curricula as examples because the behavioral method is the same for both.

One time-worn objective that many teachers set for their pupils is "to become responsible citizens." The first questions that should come to mind in order to bring the behavioral method into use are: "What exactly is a responsible citizen?" and "How will both the teacher and the learner know when this objective has been learned?" "Responsible citizenship" can be translated into some of its behavioral components. Let us suppose that in a particular class, problems of good citizenship revolve around two major areas of behavior: (1) fighting about who was first in line for drinks, recess, and so forth; and (2) ridiculing and ostracizing particular children in the class. To deal with the first problem area, objectives to teach social behavior can be stated as "to line up at the water fountain according to a prearranged plan in which every child has an opportunity to be first." If the objective is made explicit to the class, and if consequences are placed on behavior, the teacher is able to reinforce behaviors that facilitate sharing and cooperating. In this way she is leading the children toward "responsible citizenship" by dealing with a specific curriculum and objectives. In the second instance the behavioral objectives can be written, for example, "to praise classmates and to include everyone in games and activities." From this statement, too, both the teacher and the children know what is expected of them, the teacher has the opportunity to arrange events that will facilitate cooperation, and the children can be reinforced for particular behaviors or for approximations to the terminal behaviors the teacher wants the learner to display.

DEVELOPING SPECIFIC TEACHING STRATEGIES: CURRICULUM AND OBJECTIVES

Specific teaching strategies can be developed similarly if the teacher is primarily interested in cognitive development and the cultivation of scholarship. Instead of defining the objective loosely, such as "to teach children how to think," a behavioral objective and curriculum can be developed with the objective translated as "to have children differentiate among statements that are (1) factual, (2) based on inference, and (3) express values." Once objectives have been stated in such terms, specific to behavior, curriculum materials follow naturally: the teacher can make up lists of statements containing values, inferences, and statements of fact; pupils can be taught to differentiate among the three by analyzing compositions, television programs, films, and other materials of like character; they can learn when it is appropriate to use which kind of statement, and the teacher can use reinforcement procedures to help them become skilled in the appropriate use of the three.

Setting Objectives in the Basic Curricula

Even in subjects so basic as reading and writing and arithmetic some teachers have difficulty translating their long-term goals, such as "to learn how to read," into behavioral objectives such as "to learn how to read paragraphs of specific texts and answer questions about the main idea presented," or "to learn how to syllabicate words of three syllables or more." The more specific the objective is the easier it will be to reach, and the easier it will be to measure success in behavioral terms. Behavioral goals can be stated in a manner such as "to read a fourth grade textbook orally at the rate of 60 words a minute, making less than two oral reading errors per 100-word passage." Setting objectives so specifically will help the child and the teacher to pick the appropriate methods and materials of instruction.

If a teacher wants her pupils to "appreciate literature" she can never know if the objective has been achieved. Similarly, a child can say he "appreciates literature" without having ever read a book. Thus it is better for both if the objective is stated as "to read twenty-five books in a one-semester sequence of time and to write a plot summary for each book," which will result in the teacher and the child knowing what has to be done, and the teacher ultimately knowing if the child has read the books. If the teacher states her objective as "to appreciate a foreign culture," no one will ever know if she has succeeded; but if the same objective is put in the behavioral terms of "cooking and eating a typical Puerto Rican meal," or "reading and summarizing two articles from a foreign newspaper," both the teacher and the child will become involved in something that people from another culture are involved in daily. To the degree that the teacher can facilitate making this a positive experience and pair the experience with positive reinforcement, the child's desire to repeat the experience and to have additional experiences similar to that arranged in the classroom will be fostered.

Another important aspect of curriculum should be considered in the same light. Teaching children convergent thinking is just not enough; they should also learn how to make inferences and how to solve problems. These objectives, too, can be set up in behavioral terms, written in a manner such as "given problem X the learner will list ten different ways to solve the problem." As in any area of teaching, what is important here is that it be specified what the learner will do, what the criteria are for indicating success, and under what conditions the learner will demonstrate his mastery of the skills involved.

Setting Objectives
in Curriculum Areas
of Creativity

Curriculum areas such as creative writing and painting can also be taught through the setting of behavioral objectives and reinforcement procedures. For example, one study (Brigham, Graubard, and Stan, 1972) was made of a teacher who wanted to improve both the writing skills and the quality of stories written in her class. At first she tried to foster good writing by trying to inspire stories through presenting interesting pictures which the children could write about, telling exciting stories herself and stopping at an interesting place, then allowing the children to finish the story, and through trying to create an open and free atmosphere in the classroom. The children seldom wrote anything, and when they did the stories tended to be short (six to ten sentences in a fifth grade class), and dull and repetitive, as judged by independent raters who were ignorant of the teaching procedures used.

With randomly selected groups from within the class the teacher changed her teaching procedure and shifted her goal from "to teach children to be creative" to "to train children to increase the number of words they used in stories." A number of objectives, including "to use different words in stories," "to use new words," "to increase the number of ideas presented in a story," and other similar goals, were also set. These curriculum goals were very specific and could be easily communicated to the children in her class. She continued to try to inspire good writing in all the groups in her class by encouragement and presenting interesting stimuli. But with certain groups she shared her curriculum and social objectives and also reinforced, through a token system, the use of additional sentences, the use of different words, the use of new ideas in a story, and so forth. In addition to the quantitative improvements in the stories, independent raters, who again were ignorant of the teaching conditions used, rated the stories written under the specific curriculum and reinforcement procedures as superior to the stories written under the conditions of general curricula and general instead of specific reinforcement.

Other studies (Goetz and Baer, 1971; Goetz and Salmonson, 1972) have shown that specific aspects of painting and designing could also be developed systematically by teachers. The teaching of "creativity" is just as important as teaching reading and arithmetic.

When objectives are written behaviorally, with the result that the teacher knows what kind of behaviors she wants the child to produce, it is much easier for the teacher to arrange contingencies and the instructional materials in such a way that she can help the student to specifically master learning. Once the objectives wanted by the teacher or the child are clear, it is then a relatively simple matter to select the methods and actual curriculum to be used. If the objectives are not clear, almost any method or material will do.

PROGRAMMED MATERIAL

Good programmed material can save a teacher hours of work. However, very often programmed material will not be available to the teacher because of its cost—which is considerable in many cases—because of the delay in filling orders, or because good materials are not available for the subject matter or for the grade level at which the instruction is to take place. In addition, a problem with much of the commercial material in use is that it tends to emphasize convergent thinking or a "correct" answer, whereas one important goal of education is to promote divergent thinking and problem solving as well as learning facts and concepts. If the teacher wishes to promote creative work on the part of her pupils, it will be necessary for her to be able to create her own materials and teaching strategies. It is important, however, to review some of the principles and strengths of well-written programmed materials, so that if it is necessary to adapt already existing materials or create new ones, the principles of good teaching can be built into the materials.

Bushell's Criteria for Scoring
Curriculum Materials

Bushell (1972) says that the use of a particular textbook series is likely to have a stronger influence on the shape and form of an instructional sequence than anything else. He defines an instructional sequence as a single lesson, a unit of several lessons, a text, or even an entire set of texts. He has evolved a set of questions that can be used as a criterion for whether the curriculum lends itself to good teaching or not. The questions are as follows:

1. Does the curriculum describe the terminal behavior?
2. Does the curriculum measure the student's entry level?
3. Does the curriculum require frequent student responding?
4. Does the curriculum contain clear criteria for correct responses?
5. Does the curriculum contain check points and prescriptions?
6. Does the curriculum accommodate individual differences?

An affirmative answer to these questions is a good indicator that the curriculum materials in question can be used in behavior modification systems. More important, the materials will probably lead to greater learning on the part of the students than materials that do not require student responding, that have unclear objectives, that do not accommodate individual differences, and so on. How curriculum materials score on Bushell's criteria can be found in Table 1.

For example, if a set of readers does not measure the student's entry level, the teacher will have to go through a lengthy series of explorations with each student in her class to be certain that each child is working at a level commensurate with his prior knowledge. Algebra problems cannot be solved without a sufficient knowledge of arithmetic. In contrast, we can recall sitting inattentively in class while the teacher explained things that we already knew. Instances of inappropriate behavior abound in such circumstances. Most good programmed materials, fortunately, have pretests that check off those curriculum areas in which the child needs strengthen-

TABLE 1

BUSHELL'S RATING OF ACADEMIC MATERIALS

Criterion Measures	A	B	C	D	E	F
1. School Math—Singer's Sets & Numbers	Yes	No	Yes	Yes	Yes	Yes
2. Programmed Math	Yes	Yes	Yes	Yes	No	Yes
3. Educational Study Skills—social studies	No	Yes?	Yes	Yes	Yes	Yes
science	No	Yes?	Yes	Yes	Yes	Yes
reference skills	No	Yes?	Yes	Yes	Yes	Yes
4. Handwriting with Write & See	Yes	No	Yes	Yes	Yes	Yes
5. Programmed Reading	Yes	Yes	Yes	Yes	No	Yes
6. Gates-Peardon	Yes	No	Yes	Yes	No	Yes
7. SRA	No	Yes	Yes	Yes	Yes	Yes
8. Skillstarters	No	Yes	Yes	Yes	Yes	Yes
9. Reading Pacemakers	Yes	Yes	Yes	Yes	Yes	Yes
10. Phonics We Use	No	No	Yes	Yes	No	No
11. Specific Skill Series	Yes	No	Yes	Yes	No	Yes

Key
    Does the curriculum:
A   Describe the terminal behavior?
B   Measure the student's entry level?
C   Require frequent student responding?
D   Contain clear criteria for correct responses?
E   Contain check points and prescriptions?
F   Accommodate individual differences?

ing and those areas he has already mastered. Programmed material lends itself well to having students working at different levels. Even when classes are homogeneously grouped according to grade level, as indicated by standardized achievement test scores, there are vast differences between pupils in terms of specific curriculum aspects where they need help. Programmed material can also be used by aides and peers as well as by the teacher.

CURRICULUM MATERIAL SOURCES

Following is an annotated list of several commercial programs that have been used successfully in classrooms across the country. Table 1, page 137, rates these materials according to the criteria explicated by Bushell.

School Mathematics Series: Sets & Numbers (Reading, Mass: L. W. Singer Co.). Two series of elementary mathematics for grades K–6 and grades 7–8. Includes colorful workbooks with detachable pages, suitable for both review and drill work. Contains teachers manual with suggested activities and lessons. Also includes clearly stated objectives for each unit. Suitable for both slow, average, and gifted children.

Programmed Math (New York: McGraw-Hill Book Company, Webster Division). Includes eight colorful workbooks appropriate for reluctant readers. Contains diagnostic test, progress tests to measure improvement, and a teachers manual. Series is self-correcting, and child moves at his own pace.

Educational Study Skills Kits (Huntington, N.Y.: Educational Development Laboratories). Includes seven kits in science, seven in social studies, and seven in reference skills. Series covers grades 4–10 (3–9 according to authors). Each kit is one grade level of high interest, self-directing, individualized study skills in respective content areas.

Handwriting with Write and See (Chicago: Lyons & Carnahan, Inc.). Series of programmed texts which teaches the formation of capital and lowercase letters in Books 1–3; stresses evaluation of handwriting in Book 4; emphasizes legibility and uniformity in 5–6. Series uses specially treated paper and special pen so child gets immediate feedback on his performance. Includes teachers editions for each book plus a list of handwriting criteria.

Programmed Reading (New York: McGraw Hill Book Company; and New York, St. Louis, San Francisco: Buchanan-Sullivan Assoc. Press). A self-contained diagnostic and remedial kit designed for grades 1–6. Includes diagnostic placement test. Materials concentrate on word recognition, practice in phonics, practice with vowels. Colorful workbooks are self-instructing with slider to cover answers. Child moves at his own pace. Kit includes comprehension test. Matched high-interest readers are available.

Gates-Peardon Reading Exercises (New York: Teachers College Press, Columbia University). A set of supplementary exercises designed for grades 2–6. Includes separate booklet for general comprehension (main idea), following directions, predicting the outcome of selections at each of the four grade levels. Booklets are reusable. Series lends itself to self-directing, self-correcting skills.

SRA Comprehensive Reading Series (Chicago: Science Research Associates). Collection of high-interest reading selections with good workbooks, adequate teacher guides, and diagnostic checkout tests. Designed to cover the intermediate grades (2–6). Series has been found useful with low achievers in junior high school as comprehension skill builders.

Skillstarters (New York: Random House, Inc.). Highly motivating, individualized, game-oriented program of reading readiness that leads the child at his own pace to beginner readers and high-quality children's literature. Provides a management scheme that allows the teacher to keep track of child's diagnosed needs.

Reading Pacemakers and Skillpacers (New York: Random House, Inc.). A set of high-interest children's storybooks for grades 3–8; five packages of 10 books each. For each book there is a vocabulary card to preteach key vocabulary, a survey card to guide child, question cards, and activity cards. Includes a kit of 15 sets of color-coded, six-page cards, each set covering one comprehension skill and designed to teach and reinforce said skill.

Phonics We Use (Chicago: Lyons & Carnahan, Inc.). Supplementary program for phonemic approach. Includes seven workbooks on six levels—grades preprimer through 6. Teachers editions are available. Series is useful reinforcer when not used as developmental program. Also available are Phonics Games that may be used independently for small groups in a classroom setting. Both are suitable as teaching aids in primary grades or with older children with learning disabilities.

Specific Skill Series (Rockville Center, N.Y.: Barnell Loft). A selection of six competencies on six different grade levels labeled A–F. Skills included are following directions, getting the facts, drawing conclusions, locating the answer, getting the idea, using the context.

Using Programmed
Curriculum Material

The strengths of programmed material consist in its eliciting answers on the part of the pupil, almost literally forcing the child to respond to a given problem in such a way that his answer or approach to the problem is visible to the teacher. The pupil can then be reinforced for learning the correct answer. The more opportunity given the student for making overt responses, the greater will be the degree of mastery, not only of learning in the sense of accumulated knowledge but in the sense of actually being able to use the particular skill in a functional way.

The old adage "Practice makes perfect" has held up under the most intensive research inquiries. In making use of its recognized effectiveness, teachers need not rely on commercially produced programmed materials but can make up their own programs by cutting out sheets from old workbooks and making their own worksheets. (It is helpful to have a Xerox or rexograph machine for duplicating to facilitate building up a file of specific materials.) If, in the course of reading lessons, the teacher finds that Johnny has trouble with long and short vowels, it is immensely helpful if a set of worksheets is on hand on which to base instruction for him specific to that problem. He can practice independently on such worksheets and receive reinforcement for his newly learned skill. It is also quite helpful if the answer sheets accompany the worksheets so that the student can correct his own work immediately. When this procedure is used, it has been found helpful to put a red line under certain problems with explicit instructions given the child not to proceed past this point. When that point is reached the child calls the teacher over, and the problem is completed with the teacher present. The child is then reinforced for the correct answer, or the teacher can give the appropriate instruction necessary. Such a procedure prevents copying of answers without understanding them and indicates to both teacher and pupil how much actual learning has taken place. The rate measures discussed earlier also serve as a good check on pupil progress, particularly if individuals within the same class are compared on this measure as an indicator of relative progress.

Another principle of learning used by programmed instruction is that of pairing known things with unknown things until the unknown things are learned. For example, in teaching sight words a written noun is presented with a picture of the noun. Thus, the word "ladder" would be presented simultaneously with the diagram of a ladder; gradually the diagram is taken away from the reading card and the child begins to respond to the printed form of the word "ladder." The important principle here is that the more that old learning can be used in the building of new knowledge, the easier it will be for the child to learn the new material. Inherent in this principle is another extremely important aspect of curriculum: it should be sequential. The end product of learning long division, for example, must be built on the foundations of addition, subtraction, multiplication, and short division.

Both for purposes of sequencing learning and of stating objectives behaviorally, it is most important that the teacher and the learner as well take the trouble to break down the general skill or subject area into its component parts. Sometimes this can be done by means of end-of-chapter quizzes or by a step-by-step analysis of exactly what the student has to know in order to solve a given problem. The analysis itself, done by teacher and pupils together, will help to ensure learning.

Often standard curriculum material can be interestingly presented and can do an adequate job of teaching if the teacher and students will make an effort to add to the material. This can be done in a reading series, for example, by making up criteria tests that each student must pass in order to enter into a particular textbook series. The criteria can be as simple as that of reading a 100-word passage in a reading text with less than five oral errors and being able to answer four types of questions about the material read: a factual question, a question concerning a detail, a question concerning the main idea of the passage, and an inference-type question. Again, it is important that the criteria be stated as specifically as possible. Within such a curriculum series the teacher can also set up written questions and bring into use the red-line technique mentioned earlier—placing a red line every three or four pages and giving explicit instructions that students may not pass that line without responding correctly to teacher questions. Just a few minutes of work can be critical here, and can help both the student and the teacher immeasurably.

All of the above presupposes that the teacher knows what the objectives of her teaching are. This is true in far too few cases, and it is not mere reiteration of the earlier part of this chapter to say here that the lack of specific objectives is one of the most serious problems in teaching, for several reasons:

1. When goals are not specific, the teacher is not able to write specific lessons or arrange instructional materials in a way that will facilitate specific knowledge.
2. When goals are not specifically stated, the learner will not know what is expected of him and will give random answers, *hoping* to please the teacher rather than concentrating on the material to be learned. (It is important to note in this context that reinforcement, no matter what form it takes, must be made contingent on the amount of work completed *correctly* or an approximation of correct work; for if the reinforcement is placed only on the amount of work completed, a high percentage of errors will probably result as well, and in this way sloppy work habits are engendered.
3. Since the criteria for demonstrating learning will not be explicit, there will always be the danger that the youngster *appears* to have learned the material, but this will be just an assumption making it possible for the child to miss learning subject matter that will be a vital prerequisite for further learning. Thus, the youngster will enter into a chain of mistakes dysfunctional for him and the teacher alike.

As children progress through the grades an important part of their curriculum should be that they, too, learn how to set behavioral objectives. A good deal of research shows that children can and do learn more if they have a voice in choosing both the subject matter and the kind of reinforcement they are to receive. If students are to have a voice in choosing what they want to learn they must also be trained in how to make meaningful choices and how to be held accountable for their learning. Neither teachers nor children should be allowed to absolve themselves of the responsibility of following through on decisions about objectives, and learning should result in a definite change on the part of the learner to the effect that he can do something that he could not do before. One of the better books available describing in detail how to write behavioral objectives is that of Mager (1962), and it is recommended for both teachers and upper-grade students. It is important for teachers to give specific practice to children in this significant skill, and important for that skill to be exemplified by the teacher's own practices as well.

REVIEW QUESTIONS

1. A supervisor informed a group of first-grade teachers that she wanted them to state their objectives behaviorally. What does that mean?

2. Which of the following terms meet behavioral criteria, that is, where the learner must engage in an overt act to satisfy the criteria that the instructor has set: to know, to list, to understand, to appreciate, to write, to comprehend, to facilitate understanding, to demonstrate ability.

3. One professor said you can set behavioral objectives for trivial subjects but not for important subject matter like painting and creative writing or thinking. Was this an accurate statement on the professor's part?

4. List six criteria for curriculum which might aid in the selection of materials which will lead to good teaching practices.

5. One teacher stated that she would not use programmed material because the children just kept on going through the material and made too many mistakes. What procedure could you recommend to help her answer this problem?

6. The text mentions three potential problems that can arise when objectives are not specific in teaching. What are these three problems?

Chapter

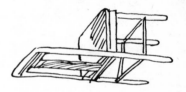

Answering Some Questions about Behavior Modification

WORKING WITH ADMINISTRATION AND STAFF

In many schools there is a tendency for some faculty members to see teachers using special methods as a specially privileged élite or as breakers of rank. You can attend to this reaction constructively by explaining your method more fully to the school staff, seeing beyond the program you are involved in. You can make consultations available to any interested teacher or perhaps arrange consultations for other staff members with one or more experts in the field. You may also wish to give workshops for other school personnel, using your own class as a demonstration class. You could also arrange to meet with the inevitable outside observers to explain the program from your point of view. You probably could participate in some consultations with other schools. Relating genuinely to school personnel on matters other than your program is also important for successful completion of your work.

Teacher and administrative resistance to your program may come from other staff members in your school. These problems can be overcome in several ways. The most forthright and intelligent solution is to try to reeducate those teachers with whom you come in contact. This can best be done by

having the teachers observe your class while you are conduct-
ing lessons in which you use behavior modification techniques
such as those described in this book. Such observations can
usually be followed up by having these teachers read one or
two articles about behavior modification, which can be found
in the *Journal of Applied Behavior Analysis*. For those colleagues who remain negative, even after repeated demonstra-
tions on your part, the best solution is to ignore their criticisms.
Their behavior will extinguish, when they realize you do not
have the time to listen to nonspecific criticisms or antagonisms.

Administrative involvement in your project will be
instrumental in holding the operation together in difficult periods. To receive administrative assistance and encouragement, you must try to be as helpful as you can in every area
of your competency. Administrators must also be reinforced to
maintain their behavior. Meetings should be scheduled regu-
larly with the school principal, and the program should keep
him informed of every step of the operation.

Another factor that is especially helpful is that whenever and wherever school action and success of program personnel can be published or communicated for project-related
work, they should be. The efforts of teachers are often re-
doubled following such public recognition.

As noted in Chapter 1, behavior modification has caused
quite a stir in education circles. Many questions and criticisms
have been leveled at behavior modification—some justified,
some totally unwarranted. If you decide to use any of the systems in this book it would be wise if you were familiar with the
questions and some of the replies to them. This chapter will
answer some of the most frequently asked questions.

ANSWERS TO QUESTIONS ABOUT BEHAVIOR MODIFICATION

1. Probably the question most often asked—and one
frequently couched in the negative—is, "But aren't you
really bribing the child to work?" You can respond to this ques-

tion in several ways. First, bribery is a negative term, that takes its meaning from an act that in most cases is unlawful. Learning, the act that we are primarily discussing, the one we wish the child to do, is neither unlawful nor negative. Learning is the most sought-after result of teaching. Children earn the reinforcers only after they have used learning behaviors. If you wish to state that we are giving things to children for learning, that is correct. However, do not call it bribery. After all, you go to work and are reinforced by paychecks with which you can buy other commodities. Is that also bribery?

2. This raises a different question: "Why do children need things? Why do children have to be reinforced with material objects in order to learn?" Let us draw an analogy to a teacher who is on a diet. A dieter is often given pills by a doctor with which he can reduce and lose weight. We might now ask the question, why give him pills? We give the dieter pills to help him emit a specified behavior and reach a specified goal. He is given pills because he cannot reduce on his own. In the same way we give children reinforcers, material objects, because they cannot work initially without them. They cannot reduce their level of inappropriate behavior without a "pill," which in our case is a reinforcer. When they are given reinforcers they are able to start reducing and to strengthen the behaviors necessary for such reduction—in the same way that a teacher, after losing weight, is often able to maintain a certain weight without pills, particularly if he is given reinforcement for being thin and can do things (have more dates, stamina and so forth) that he couldn't do before.

We can think of another analogy that clarifies the role of behavior modification techniques used in the classroom. To build a strong and sturdy building we require brick, and mortar to hold the bricks together. Without the mortar the building will collapse. In the same way, reinforcers can be looked on as being mortar for the child's behavioral repertoire. Without the mortar the appropriate behaviors that have been built up will disintegrate and extinguish. By giving a child a reinforcer we are cementing together his behavioral repertoire until it can stand on its own.

3. Another question concerns the long-term effects of a behavior modification program: "What happens to the children after your program has been completed? Do the children become addicted to reinforcers? Will they be able to work without them when they are put into another class that is not "special"?

As you know, all behavior is maintained by reinforcement. If an individual is put into a new environment in which appropriate behaviors are ignored or punished, these behaviors will most probably extinguish. If a teacher in this new environment decides to reinforce, through attention, a child's *inappropriate* behaviors, there is no reason to believe that the individual's *appropriate* behavior rate will increase. Quite to the contrary, a teacher who reinforces inappropriate behavior can expect nothing but increased inappropriate behavior from the child. Hence, when considering the long-term effects of your program, you must understand that there can be no long-term effects unless the behaviors you have conditioned are maintained by reinforcers in the new environment. If the new teacher reinforces behaviors, they will be maintained. If she does not reinforce the behaviors, no miracles should be expected; the behaviors will extinguish. This is not a magical system. It is based on experimentation and observation, and one cannot expect results that are not based on the principles of behavior.

4. Other questions frequently asked concern restrictions of freedom imposed on children by behavior modification systems. "Don't you program the child to such a degree that he has no free choice? Are you really teaching thinking and logic and creativity? After all, there is no creativity if you don't allow the child the freedom of choice."

Creativity can come only after the basic building blocks have been laid. A child cannot be creative if he does not have the tools to be creative with. One goal of a behavior modification system is to give the child these basic skills to cement together a repertoire with which he can interact with his environment and create a new environment and new behaviors. In a sense all systems of teaching, whether they are called open-corridor or Montessori or programmed instruction, are all restrictive. They are restrictive in the sense that they do not allow the child to do *anything* that he wants. Most events the child enters into are planned for him—that is, a child who enters a math lesson and is in the third grade cannot be given calculus. That child must first have the prerequisites before he can get to calculus. So we present to the child those stimuli and those lessons that are at his level. In that sense each child is programmed. Each child is presented with lessons and materials he is able to do at that time and that will broaden his repertoire.

The child being taught according to many of the systems discussed in this book can be given the freedom to choose from among many lessons and activities. This is not a restrictive system, but one that encourages freedom of choice and that nurtures learning.

There is no reason why creative activity cannot be fostered using a reinforcement system. If you specify your terminal and interim objectives, it is possible to reinforce those behaviors that lead to your programmed goal. Your objectives can be painting, playing music, writing, as well as reading, arithmetic computation, or social behavior.

5. Many a teacher we've talked with has been impressed by the results of this program. One question they often ask goes like this: "Granted, Eli and Jimmy and Dorothy are really improved, but how do I know it was the program and not the teacher? The teacher in this instance could have done the same thing without the program."

This question can only be answered from a scientific and research point of view. There are research techniques for evaluating just such a problem, and they are best exemplified in articles that can be found in the *Journal of Applied Behavior Analysis*. Basically, these methodologies involve comparing the teacher and the class to their own baseline performance. Class progress can be measured under a traditional method, a behavior modification method, and again under a traditional method. Most studies find that children do better, *even under the same teacher,* when behavior modification procedures are used. The techniques delineated in this book can make any teacher a "better" teacher. She can be a better teacher because she can now deal with her own and her students' behaviors with effective methods. Research has clearly corroborated this point.

6. "I know it works with children who have problems and need help, but what good is it for those children without such problems and who are working at grade level or even above it?"

Behavior modification is not a technique solely for problem children and problem adults. As indicated in the text, teachers' behaviors can also be modified with similar techniques.

The specification of curricula materials at the student's appropriate level is a necessity regardless of the teacher's theoretical bent. Behavior modification technology does offer an ongoing assessment of the effect of your curricula materials. As such, it is difficult to argue with the techniques.

So, it comes down to reinforcing children. Even children of above average ability must be reinforced. If you are able to program this reinforcement, then the child is no longer subject to the whims of nature but can be given a better educational environment in which to use his abilities. There can be little argument about effect—even for the above average student. The only question is how well can we program the environment.

To this point we have discussed the principles of behavioral analysis, behavioral management techniques, classroom observation schedules, and curriculum integration. Facility with all four components are requisites for successful programs in the classroom. After your program has been functioning for a while, you will probably receive requests from colleagues and visitors to observe your classroom and to learn more about the workings of your program. You may also receive requests from your supervisors to train other staff members to use these systems. You may wish to use this handbook as reading material for educators, parents, or aides with whom you discuss these principles and techniques. Some people learn more easily from observing a system in operation than from reading about it. Open your door and let them in.

Appendixes

Appendix A

Available Backup Reinforcers

Monitor job (plants, animals, milk, clean sinks, blackboard, hold door for lineup, and similar ones).
First on line.
Free time.
Extra art period (music, science, and so forth).
Work with microscope.
Work with typewriter.
Acting (drama).
Extra work with teacher.
Present puppet show to class.
Show special film strips.
Reading a story to class.
Private discussion with teacher.
Appointment with other school personnel.
Use of special crayons.
Free period in library.
Class trip.
Learning to write script.
Team leader.
Teacher attention.
Watering plants.
Keeping classroom records of behavior modification program.
Learning to graph.
Teacher's aide at entrance to classroom activities programs.
Entrance into skills program (see p. 80 for survival kit).
Honors' lists for best work of week.
Working with a friend in class for specified time.
Outside-of-school reinforcers (see p. 70).
Picture on bogus money.
Use of special equipment in gym.

Appendix B

Chapter 1

1. Carol's mother was following the guidelines laid out in this chapter. She set up her objectives so that the reinforcers were to be delivered contingently upon a specified performance by Carol. This type of example demonstrates the benefit of bringing parents into the learning process because they have control over a great number of reinforcers that might be beyond the reach of the teacher. In this example Carol's completed homework assignments will probably be helpful in reinforcing classroom behavior.

2. The doll was being given on a noncontingent basis. That, is the teacher was agreeing to give Vivian the doll even though Vivian had not yet finished her lesson. As a result, Vivian may have learned that she does not have to complete her lessons to get rewarded. It is very likely that in the future Vivian will continue to ask the teacher for a reward prior to completion of her assignments.

3. The principal could have made several possible suggestions to the teacher. Among them are: (1) yelling at a child in an attempt to control him may be effective for a short period of time, but will not have any long-term effects, (2) yelling in the classroom by the teacher tends to be disruptive for others who are working, (3) it would be possible to handle this type of situation in various other ways; for example, you could set up a contingency for such behavior and try to extinguish it by ignoring it or reinforcing an incompatible behavior.

4. The teacher did not follow the guideline that states that you should be consistent and systematic in the modification of any behavior. That is, be consistent in your criterion for reinforcement and consistent in your methods of treating any child.

5. The inference is correct. While hitting a child may have the desirable short-term effect of suppression of the child's behavior and the release of your own anger, it probably will not be successful over the long term and could indeed adversely affect your relationship with the child.

6. It would be wise of the teacher to remind the mother of the guideline concerning successive approximations to a final behavior. Because this boy had a history of inappropriate behaviors in school it would seem logical that he would not turn into the "model student" overnight. However, it should be pointed out that interim goals could be set which he probably could meet without too much difficulty, and that gradually the objectives would be made more demanding.

7. This intervention has many faults. First, reinforcers should be given contingent upon a specified behavior and should not be available at all times of the day. The dimensions for distributing reinforcers have been reviewed in this chapter and indicate clearly that the time, the place, and the distributor of the reinforcers must be clearly specified. In addition, since food and toys are being used by the teacher as potential reinforcers during the entire day it is conceivable that their value as reinforcers may diminish due to satiation. In addition, toys and candy may not be reinforcing for some children in your class. It is advisable to discover what the particular reinforcers are for each of your students.

8. Some conditioned reinforcers are: points, stars, checks, bogus money, points in a savings book, tokens. Cost-free backup reinforcers will probably be specific to each class; however, here are some that are generally available in most classes: extra free time, use of a typewriter, being a monitor, extra art period, an opportunity to do extra work for additional points, extra gym time, being the leader of a group or team, a commendation note to the parents, etc.

9. The use of punishment is a technique that requires careful supervision and the specification of the target behaviors that will be punished. You must have good reasons for not using some other technique. It has been advised that you receive permission from a principal or a group of your peers to use these techniques. Punishment, unlike the other techniques discussed in this book, can cause severe adverse reactions that you may not be able to control, and thus you are advised to heed the precautions given in this chapter.

10. It cannot be emphasized often enough that reinforcers must be given on a contingent basis if they are to be effective in

modifying the targeted behavior. A reinforcer is defined by its ability to increase the probability of behavior. If the targeted behavior does not increase then either the reinforcer is not being given contingently or else it is an inadequate one. It should also be noted that the distribution of reinforcers should follow the guidelines enumerated in this chapter as to the time, place, and condition of distribution.

Chapter 2

1. Strengths: (a) Tokens are portable and can be rewarded to the children in a variety of settings; (b) the child can be reinforced immediately for appropriate behavior without interrupting lessons; (c) tokens can be used to take advantage of a variety of wants for many individuals because they can be exchanged for so many things; (d) tokens are less subject to satiation states; (e) tokens give concrete evidence to the child that he has accomplished something. Disadvantages: (a) tokens can be lost or stolen; (b) tokens can be dropped and make noise.

2. (a) Identifying the behaviors to be altered in such a way that they are objective and measurable, and in such a manner that both child and teacher will know when changes have occurred. (b) Applying the tokens in a specific time relationship with the behavior. (c) Finding backup reinforcers which will affect the behavior to be changed, and (d) utilizing appropriate curriculum.

3. A child could falsify the number of correct answers he had, either consciously or through carelessness. The child would then be reinforced for misrepresentation. Make sure you know what you are reinforcing.

4. By presetting prices you avoid a tendency to price your reinforcers according to how many tokens the children have earned. By making the prices public you avoid having a dole system where children get things according to your benevolence. With preset prices and an explicit ratio of reinforcement to work, the child gets what he earns.

5. One way is to increase the value of the backup reinforcers. This will increase the value of the tokens and make children guard their tokens more carefully. If you are aware that a specific individual or individuals are stealing the tokens you could give them a differently shaped token which would prevent them from using others. Another way to handle this problem is to move to a grid system where you, and only

you, possess a unique stamp which the children cannot duplicate.

6. No, but with a little bit of experience you can make good guesses. In the final analysis, reinforcers are defined empirically by their effect on behavior, and only the child can tell you what he finds reinforcing. He tells you this by his behavior and not by his words.

7. (a) Students do not receive sufficient reinforcement. Your goals are too high and/or you are not catching them being "good." (b) The curriculum is too hard and/or aversive to them. (c) The backup reinforcers have little value for the children.

Chapter 3

1. (a) Specified behaviors.
    (b) Specified duration or amount of behaviors.
    (c) Specified contingent reinforcers.

2. (a) Setting timer and giving points to the children who return to work on time.
    (b) Giving bonus points to the children who begin their academic work on time and making it worthwhile to start these activities.

3. No. Reinforcers are quite idiosyncratic and while most children might prefer gym to reading there will be a substantial number who prefer reading over gym. Observe the individual and work with their desires, not the desires of the average student.

4. The word good must be better defined. Since it has such a wide latitude of interpretation, the teacher should make the criteria explicit so that both she and the children are in agreement on its meaning.

5. One possibility would be to initially alternate high and low preference events. For example, let us assume that arithmetic was a low preference event and dramatics was a high preference event. Access to dramatics could be made contingent on the completion of arithmetic. If gym was a more preferred event than reading, gym could follow reading and the teacher could eventually chain the subjects together so that the children had to complete two low preference events to gain access to a high preference event. Eventually the schedule could be worked so that children had to complete all of their academic assignments to gain access to other areas.

6. There is no evidence that any general treatment helps specific performance. The most practical way to treat the arithmetic difficulty is to directly teach, and reinforce arithmetic knowledge.

7. The teacher should not allow Gregory to visit him after school, at least not until Gregory fulfills his part of the bargain. However, the teacher should note that there is a problem that needs to be corrected. Perhaps the academic work is too hard or there are too many problems to complete. Perhaps the child is not really interested in visiting the teacher after school. The teacher should tinker around with the assignment and the reinforcer until he finds an effective combination. It is easier to blame Gregory, but that won't be as helpful as correcting the situation.

8. It can bring some additional backup reinforcers into play. It is sometimes helpful to the student to know that his parents are aware of the specifics of his or her classroom behavior and academic progress. It can help parents learn how to reinforce the good things that a child does.

Chapter 4

1. Graph of Kathy's and teacher's behavior:

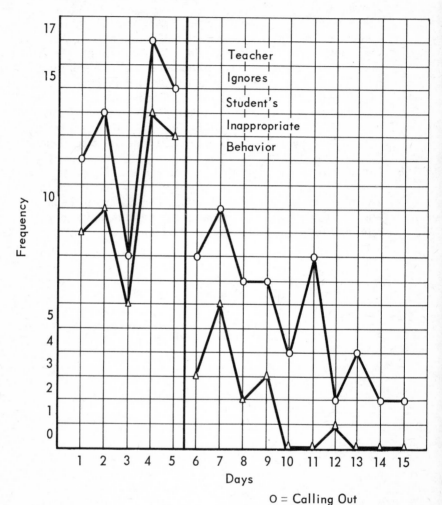

Teacher
Ignores
Student's
Inappropriate
Behavior

O = Calling Out
Δ = Teacher Attention

KATHY'S BEHAVIOR: Calling Out

TEACHER'S BEHAVIOR: Responding to Calling Out

2. (1) baseline
   (2) teacher's behavior

(3) ignore–extinguish
(4) extinguish
(5) a, b, c, d, e, j

Chapter 5

1. When an objective is stated behaviorally it contains a criteria measure which the learner must display to satisfy the teacher that the objective has been accomplished. The behavior display has to be overt, unambiguous, and specific, and the learner must engage in some observable act or leave some observable product such as written answers.
2. To list, to write, to demonstrate ability.
3. No. Behavioral objectives can be set for skills such as creative writing, painting, and thinking if these skills are broken into component parts. For example, part of "thinking" consists of differentiating between those statements which are factual and those which are based on inference. Using behavioral objectives, a specific curriculum can be set up to help learners distinguish between different kinds of arguments and statements and specific criteria can be used to judge how well the learner has been able to apply these skills.
4. (a) Does the curriculum describe the terminal behaviors?
   (b) Does the curriculum measure the student's entry level?
   (c) Does the curriculum require frequent student responding?
   (d) Does the curriculum contain clear criteria for correct responses?
   (e) Does the curriculum contain check points and prescriptions?
   (f) Does the curriculum accommodate individual differences?
5. The red line procedure, where a line is placed under certain problems with explicit instructions to the child not to proceed past that point, has been found to be helpful. When that red line is reached the child calls the teacher over and the problem is completed with the teacher present. Such a procedure prevents copying of answers without understanding them and indicates to both teacher and pupil how much actual learning has taken place.
6. (a) When goals are not specified the teacher is not able to write appropriate lessons or arrange instructional materials in such a way that specific knowledge will be facilitated.

(b) When goals are not specifically stated the learner will not know what is expected and/or correct.

(c) Without criteria measures learners may appear to have learned, but may not be able to concretely apply it.

References

Ayllon, T., and Azrin, N. *The Token Economy: A Motivational System for Therapy and Rehabilitation.* New York: Appleton, 1968.

Barrish, H. H., Saunders, M., and Wolf, M. M. Good behavior game: effects of individual contigencies for group consequences on disruptive behavior in the classroom. *Journal of Applied Behavior Analysis,* 1969, 2, 119–124.

Becker, W. C., Madsen, C. H., Arnold, R., and Thomas, D. R. The contingent use of teacher attention and praise in reducing classroom behavior problems. *Journal of Special Education,* 1967, 1, 287–307.

Brigham, T. A., Graubard, P. S., and Stan, A. Analysis of the effects of sequential reinforcement contigencies on aspects of composition. *Journal of Applied Behavior Analysis,* 1972, 5, 421–430.

Buros, O. K. (ed.). *The Seventh Mental Measurements Yearbook.* Highland Park, N.J.: Gryphon, 1972.

Bushell, D., Jr. *Classroom Behavior.* Englewood Cliff, N.J.: Prentice-Hall, 1973.

Bushell, D., Jr., and Brigham, T. A. Classroom token systems as technology. *Educational Technology,* 1971, II, 14–18.

Goetz, E. M., and Baer, D. M. Descriptive social reinforcement of "creative" block building by young children. In E. A. Ramp and B. L. Hopkins (ed.), *A New Direction for Education: Behavior Analysis, 1971.* The University of Kansas: Support and Development Center for Follow Through, 1971, pp. 72–79.

169

Goetz, E. M., and Salmonson, M. M. The Effect of General and Descriptive Reinforcement in "Creativity" in Easel Painting in C. Semb (ed.), *Behavior Analysis and Education, 1972.* The University of Kansas: Support and Development Center for Follow Through. Department of Human Development, 1972, pp. 53–61.

Graubard, P. S., Rosenberg, H., and Miller, M. B. Student applications of behavior modification to teachers and environments or ecological approaches to social deviancy. In E. A. Ramp and B. L. Hopkins (eds.), *A New Direction for Education: Behavior Analysis,* 1971. The University of Kansas: Support and Development Center for Follow Through, 1971, pp. 80–101.

Mager, R. F. *Preparing Instructional Objectives.* Palo Alto, Calif.: Fearon, 1962.

O'Leary, K. D., and Becker, W. The effects of the intensity of a teacher's reprimands on children's behavior. *Journal of School Psychology,* 1969, 7, 8–11.

O'Leary, K. D., and Drabman, R. Token reinforcement programs in the classroom: A review. *Psychological Bulletin,* 1971, 75, 379–98.

Skinner, B. F. *The Technology of Teaching.* New York: Appleton, 1968.

Spence, I. Counting the teacher reactions to pupil behaviors: A tool for teacher training. Unpublished doctoral dissertation. Yeshiva University, 1972.

Thomas, D., Becker, W., and Armstrong, M. Production and elimination of disruptive classroom behavior by systematically varying teacher's behavior. *Journal of Applied Behavior Analysis,* 1968, *1,* 35–45.

Williams, R., and Anandam, K. *Cooperative Classroom Management.* Columbus, Ohio: Merrill, 1973.

INDEX